D0475934

The Real RUDOLPH

A NATURAL HISTORY OF THE REINDEER

TILLY SMITH

SUTTON PUBLISHING

To
My Dad

First published in the United Kingdom in 2006 by
Sutton Publishing Limited · Phoenix Mill
Thrupp · Stroud · Gloucestershire · GL5 2BU

British Library Cataloguing in Publication Data
A catalogue record for this book is available from the British Library.

ISBN 0-7509-4283-5

Typeset in 10.5/14pt Melior.
Typesetting and origination by
Sutton Publishing Limited.
Printed and bound in England by
J.H. Haynes & Co. Ltd, Sparkford.

Contents

Late summer in the Cairngorms, Scotland, and the reindeer calves are cooling off at a water hole.

Acknowledgements and Picture Credits

Writing *The Real Rudolph* would never have been possible if there were not people to help reduce the workload of my 'day job', reindeer herding and running the Reindeer Company. To this end, a heartfelt thank you to Alan and Catriona.

My first-hand experiences with reindeer have found me as far a field as Outer Mongolia and Arctic Sweden. Not being a seasoned traveller, visiting Outer Mongolia was always going to be a daunting affair. To this end Alex and Jess made fantastic travel companions and together we coped with everything Mongolian life threw at us. Our travels through Mongolia on horseback were made all the more enjoyable by our Mongolian guide Butsuuri, cook Merga and horseman Hunda.

On our various trips to Swedish Lapland Alan and I were guests of the Utsi brothers, Per Ola, Jussa and John Erling. Their hospitality was unsurpassed and our time there just made us want to return again and again.

The Real Rudolph has a feast of wonderful photos of reindeer and caribou from all over the world and to this end I am grateful to the following sources for permission to reproduce images from their collections: Mark Hicken, p. vi; Alex Smith, Sirkas Productions, pp. ix, 11, 14, 27, 36, 46, 69, 88, 90, 93, 94, 96, 125, 157, 159; Ruth Ives, p. 4; B. & C. Alexander, Arctic Photo, pp. 16–17, 18, 42, 47, 56–7, 62, 63, 72–3, 78, 80, 165; Laurie Campbell, p. 32; Niall Benvie, p. 35; Paul Hastings, p. 39; British Antarctic Survey, pp. 100–1; Alaska State Library, p. 106; Royal Navy Submarine Museum, p. 110; The Reindeer Company Ltd, pp. 114, 116–17, 118, 160; Heather Angel, p. 119; Richard Ansett, p. 144; Nigel Housden, p. 167.

Shekel, a Christmas reindeer from the Cairngorm reindeer herd, posing in the winter sun. 'Rudolph', the most famous reindeer of all, has been depicted in numerous ways but invariably nothing like the real thing.

Preface: Love at First Sight

My passion for natural history and in particular deer stems from my childhood as the daughter of the local doctor in a Hertfordshire village. My Dad was and still is a great enthusiast of the natural world and he passed his enthusiasm on to me while I was still very young. One of the 'old school', he was, however, most disappointed when I elected to read Zoology at university. His reaction to my decision was, to say the least, rather negative. I can remember his words to this day: 'There are only three professions worth following, medicine, law and architecture.' He did not regard zoology as a worthy topic to study.

All through my childhood we were immersed in the deer world. As a local expert on the small muntjac deer, my Dad was regularly brought dead or half-dead specimens that had been knocked down on the road, caught up in farm machinery or found and wrongly assumed to have been 'abandoned' by their mothers. Any we could we nursed back to health, bottle fed fawns, ate the casualties for supper and took part in live catching exercises with nets around the woods of Hertfordshire to satisfy my Dad's desire to study them.

Despite my father's negative attitude towards zoology, I was enough of a rebel to persist with it for my degree, and so in October 1978 I began a three-year honours degree at Bristol University. But as the final year came to a close I wondered what on earth I was going to do next. It looked as if my father's dire remarks about useful degrees were coming true.

However, in my dim and distant past I remembered a rather eccentric lady coming to my Dad's local Natural History Society Christmas meeting to talk about reindeer. As was the normal protocol, the guest speaker was invited to our house for supper prior to the meeting. As always, my Mum had put on a great spread for supper in the dining room where we normally entertained guests. It was a wild night, in the days when snow was not uncommon in Hertfordshire. But despite the weather conditions, the speaker Dr Ethel John Lindgren arrived very promptly. Dr Lindgren was an expert on reindeer. In 1952 she and her husband Mikel Utsi, a Swedish Sami, had successfully reintroduced reindeer to Scotland, and they devoted the latter half of their lives to ensuring the project was a success. Always one to make the most of the occasion, Dr Lindgren arrived extremely well dressed from top to toe, the crowning glory being, as I remember, a diamond tiara on her head. In contrast, we were by comparison in decidedly casual wear. On greeting Dr Lindgren, my Dad commented on the deteriorating weather conditions and expressed his hope that there would be plenty of people for the meeting. Dr Lindgren replied, 'I do hope so, Doctor Dansie.'

Dr Lindgren obviously made a lasting impression on me and, although I could not remember a thing she had said about reindeer on the night, I decided in my last few months at university to write to her and offer my services as a volunteer to work with her herd of reindeer in Scotland. The subsequent interview at her house in Cambridge turned out to be more of an interrogation and she made the instant decision to offer me the job of Reindeer Keeper, although I don't recall the mention of any wages. My impression was that there was a keeper up there already looking after the herd, but that he was no good and so I would probably end up caring for the reindeer myself. Whatever that meant.

So it was that in June 1981 I drove north for the first time to meet my destiny. Eidart was the first reindeer I set eyes on. A 6-year-old female reindeer, she was in the paddocks beside Reindeer House with her calf. My instant impression was one of size – Eidart seemed so small, and not what I imagined at all.

People often ask me how I came to the reindeer initially and my usual reply is 'fate'. That summer of 1981 was without a doubt 'meant to be'. Very soon after my arrival I fell in love with the reindeer, the mountains and the reindeer keeper – not necessarily in that order, of course. Nearly a quarter of a century on and the love affair is as strong as ever.

A reindeer calf from a Tsataan camp in Outer Mongolia makes friends with the author – 'I felt sure my life with reindeer was "meant to be"'.

My experiences with reindeer have almost all been 'hands on'. Through their life cycle, being with them for nearly twenty-five years, I have learnt about dietary requirements, handling and individual characters. Over the years I have dipped into various books about reindeer, their biology, physiology and veterinary aspects, always in connection with improving the daily management of the herd, but it was not until recently that I have had the time to research deeper into the world of reindeer. Raising two children, jointly running the Cairngorm reindeer herd, helping on our farm and keeping up with the many projects that my husband Alan has simultaneously on the go have hampered any opportunity to take my love of reindeer further than the bounds of our own herd.

Much of their physiology I already know, indeed I suspect sometimes I know better than the so-called experts! But their prehistory, their interaction with man and the extent to which man to this day still relies on reindeer has only now come to my attention, vastly broadening my depth of reindeer knowledge. No doubt reindeer in some manner or form will occupy the rest of my life, whether it be the daily care of our herd, encountering reindeer elsewhere around the globe or simply as part of my dreams. Reindeer will always hold a very special place in my heart. I hope I can impart some of my enthusiasm for them to my readers.

ONE

Who is Rudolph?

It is Christmas Eve and a party of people have joined me on the mountainside to visit part of the Cairngorm reindeer herd. With the group gathered round I extol the virtues of reindeer, explaining how they can survive in temperatures similar to a deep freeze and how their placid nature stems from thousands of years of domestication by man. While the group of reindeer patiently wait to be fed, I ask the visitors if anyone has any questions. Encouraged by his mother, a young lad pipes up, 'Which one is Rudolph?' 'Well actually,' I reply, 'Rudolph's not here today. He's higher up in the mountains resting in preparation for the busy night ahead, but I have got some of his friends here instead.' 'Oh,' he replies, a little disappointed by Rudolph's absence. He perseveres though and, looking quizzically at the reindeer, asks, 'How do they fly?' With a suitably serious expression on my face, I reply, 'Only Santa Claus knows the real answer to your question but I think it is something to do with the magic stardust that he sprinkles on the reindeers' favourite food, lichen.' Then, with the flying abilities of reindeer satisfactorily explained, I proceed with the rest of the visit.

A Visit from St Nicholas

Rudolph was not the first flying reindeer; indeed, he was not created until 1939. In fact the first reference to flying reindeer in modern times comes from a poem written by Clement C. Moore, a classical scholar and poet, who in 1822 wrote a poem about the night before Christmas for his children. An expert on folklore, in particular of the Dutch, German and Scandinavian immigrants who had settled in the United States, Moore blended aspects of St Nicholas, the patron saint of travel, children and sailors with the Dutch equivalent Sinterklaas, the pagan mid-winter festival concerned with appeasing the gods with feasts and festivities, and Norse mythology. From this concoction he wrote the following poem:

'Twas the night before Christmas, when all through the house
Not a creature was stirring, not even a mouse;
The stockings were hung by the chimney with care,
In hopes that St Nicholas soon would be there.

The children were nestled all snug in their beds,
While visions of sugarplums danced in their heads;
And Mama in her kerchief and I in my cap,
Had just settled down for a long winter's nap,

When out on the lawn there rose such a clatter,
I sprang from my bed to see what was the matter.
Away to the window I flew like a flash,
Tore open the shutters and threw up the sash.

The moon on the breast of the new-fallen snow,
Gave a lustre of midday to objects below;
When, what to my wondering eyes should appear,
But a miniature sleigh and eight tiny reindeer,

With a little old driver so lively and quick,
I knew in a moment it must be St Nick.
More rapid than eagles his coursers they came,
And he whistled and shouted and called them by name –

'Now, Dasher! Now, Dancer! Now, Prancer and Vixen!
On, Comet! On, Cupid! On Donner and Blitzen!
To the top of the porch, to the top of the wall!
Now, dash away! Dash away! Dash away all!'

As dry leaves before the wild hurricanes fly,
When they meet with an obstacle mount to the sky,

So up to the housetop the coursers they flew,
With a sleigh full of toys – and St Nicholas too;

And then in a twinkling, I heard on the roof
The prancing and pawing of each little hoof.
As I drew in my head and was turning around,
Down the chimney St Nicholas came with a bound.

He was dressed all in fur from his head to his foot,
And his clothes were all tarnished with ashes and soot.
A bundle of toys he had flung on his back,
And he looked like a peddler just opening his pack.

His eyes how they twinkled! His dimples how merry!
His cheeks were like roses, his nose like a cherry!
His droll little mouth was drawn up like a bow,
And his beard on his chin was as white as the snow!

The stump of a pipe he held tight in his teeth,
And the smoke it encircled his head like a wreath.
He had a broad face and a little round belly
That shook when he laughed like a bowl full of jelly.

He was chubby and plump – a right jolly old elf,
And I laughed when I saw him in spite of myself.
A wink of his eye and a twist of his head,
Soon gave me the know I had nothing to dread.

He spoke not a word, but went straight to his work,
And filled all the stockings, then turned with a jerk,
And laying his finger aside of his nose,
And giving a nod, up the chimney he rose.

He sprang to his sleigh, to his team gave a whistle,
And away they flew like the down of a thistle.
But I heard him exclaim as he drove out of sight,
'Merry Christmas to all and to all a Good Night!'

Clement C. Moore, 1822

So where did Clement Moore get the idea that St Nick may arrive on a sleigh pulled by 'eight tiny reindeer'? In Norse mythology Odin, the warrior god of wisdom and war, rode a horse called Sleipner, a fine young stallion with eight legs born to Loki, the god of Hokey Pokey and one of the world's major trickster gods. Perhaps the combination of this eight-legged beast, a large amount of magic and the ancient Finnish legend of 'Old Man Winter', who drove the reindeer down from the mountains into the lowlands with the coming of cold weather, had inspired Moore. Certainly Odin was a god who presided over those who deserved reward or punishment. Riding his fine beast and clad in a large cloak and wide-brimmed hat, he visited the Norse people dispensing punishments and rewards as appropriate.

Wherever Clement C. Moore gathered his ideas for the poem, it became an instant success across America and remains a popular children's Christmas poem to this day, republished and recited in various forms. But in recent times the original eight reindeer – Dasher, Dancer, Prancer, Vixen, Comet, Cupid, Donner and Blitzen – have been joined by another, perhaps the best known of all.

Rudolph the Red-Nosed Reindeer

Rudolph was created by the Montgomery Ward group of department stores in the United States. They commissioned author Robert L. May to come up with a Christmas story as a promotional gimmick for their customers in 1939. The story

goes that May based his story 'Rudolph the Red-Nosed Reindeer' on the Hans Christian Andersen fairy tale 'The Ugly Duckling'. It was about a young reindeer who was very different to the rest of the herd because of his red nose. Indeed, in the original story Rudolph was not one of Santa's reindeer and he lived in a reindeer village that was not necessarily at the North Pole. The story was created around the time of alcohol prohibition, when the subject of alcoholism and drunkards was taboo. A red nose was often a sign of drunkenness and the department-store managers were nervous that a reindeer with a red nose would be unsuitable for a Christmas tale. But their concerns were unfounded and in the very first year of publication Montgomery Ward handed out 2.5 million copies. During the Second World War printing was suspended for several years, but even so some 6 million copies had been distributed by 1946.

The Ninth Flying Reindeer

In 1949 a song about Rudolph the Red-Nosed Reindeer was recorded by Gene Autry. It sold 2 million copies and has gone on to be one of the best-selling Christmas songs of all time. The lyrics were written by Johnny Marks and there were substantial differences from May's original story. In the song Marks brought together the original eight reindeer from Clement Moore's poem with Rudolph as their leader; his nose lit up the sky and guided them through the foggy night. Everyone in the Western world knows who Rudolph is on Christmas Eve when he helps Santa deliver the presents to all the children. But who is he, or she, for the rest of the year?

A Family of Deer

There are at least forty different species of deer spread across the world, occupying a vast range of ecological niches. The smallest member of the family is the Pudu, which frequents the forested slopes of the Andes, while the largest is the moose, which inhabits the forests and marsh lands of northern Europe, Siberia, Canada, Alaska and the state of Wyoming in the United States. Rudolph is to be found living to the south of Santa's home at the North Pole, in the tundra, mountains and woodlands of the arctic and sub-arctic areas of the northern hemisphere. His scientific name is *Rangifer tarandus* and he is the only arctic species of deer. Famous for long migrations, large herd size, a predilection for lichen and as a food source for wolves and man, Rudolph is a deer whose range covers one-fifth of the earth's surface and whose total world population is approximately 6 million. He goes by the name of reindeer in north Scandinavia and Russia, after the Lappish word 'reino', meaning reindeer calf, while in the North American arctic he is called caribou, a name derived from the Micmac Indian word meaning 'digger of snow'. Across Russia and north Scandinavia the vast majority of reindeer are domesticated and underpin the lifestyle of the indigenous people of these areas. However, the caribou remain completely wild.

As a general rule, male and female reindeer and caribou are referred to as bulls and cows respectively and the young are called calves. This contrasts with other species of deer, for example fallow deer, which are normally called bucks, does and fawns, and red deer, which are generally called stags, hinds and calves.

Habits and Habitat

As a member of the deer family Cervidae, Rudolph shares many features common to other species within the family. They all belong to the sub-order Ruminantia and so all deer digest their food by a process of rumination or 'chewing the cud'. This complicated process involves a combination of four separate stomach chambers between the oesophagus and the intestine and requires the services of millions of bacteria and hundreds of millions of protozoa.

During a feeding session a deer will crop as much vegetation as it needs, using its front incisors, and stores it partially chewed in the first and most capacious of the stomach chambers, the rumen. Once satisfied, he will then generally lie down to digest the food he has gathered. This part of the process involves small balls of food, or cud, being regurgitated, chewed properly using the molars and swallowed again. It then proceeds through the next three chambers, the reticulum, omasum and abomasum, and finally reaches the intestine. Throughout these phases bacteria break down the plant cellulose and starch by means of enzymes into soluble fatty acids. These bacteria are then consumed by the protozoa, which, besides digesting starch, convert plant protein into animal protein. In their turn the protozoa become available to the ruminant when they themselves are destroyed and digested further down the intestine. The whole process involves copious quantities of saliva, reproducing bacteria and protozoa and an extremely complicated stomach lining of mucous-secreting glands. During the process large quantities of methane and carbon dioxide are produced. Such activity occupies a substantial percentage of the body mass of a deer, and indeed the rumen and associated organs constitute 50 per cent of the live weight of the animal.

This type of digestion governs the daily behavioural pattern of deer. Throughout the daylight hours deer will alternate feeding with periods of resting and digesting. This can be an important survival strategy for a primary consumer that is vulnerable to predation while out feeding, but can hide itself away or gather as a group during the process of digestion. Rumination is also an extremely efficient way to digest food and extract all the goodness from a huge variety of vegetation. This has led to different members of the deer family being able to occupy a vast array of habitats, from the tundra of the frozen north to the profuse tropical rain-forests of the south.

According to the habitat they live in, different deer species vary in their habits from being basically solitary to highly gregarious. The smaller, more primitive deer, like the Pudu, tend to be solitary, only forming small family groups at certain times of year. Quite often there is bonding for life between male and female. At the other end of the evolutionary spectrum, deer species like reindeer or caribou tend to form large herds with the males claiming a harem of females during the breeding season. This polygamous reproductive strategy means there is no lasting contact between males and females after the rutting season. The reproductive success of a bull reindeer holding a harem of cows is enhanced by the attainment of a large body size, hence there is a marked size dichotomy between bulls and cows with breeding bulls being considerably bigger.

Vital Statistics

My first impression of reindeer was how small they seemed to be, and visitors to our Cairngorm herd commonly comment that they expected the animals to be bigger. I am not sure how this misconception arises but I think it may result from the fact that people confuse reindeer with the larger moose. The average reindeer stands 120cm at the shoulder and weighs anything up to 150kg. The moose by comparison is substantially bigger, at more than twice the height and weight.

The caribou of North America are on average taller and heavier than the reindeer of Eurasia, with a fully grown bull caribou being up to 50 per cent heavier than a reindeer bull. Size is mainly a reflection of the level of nutrition available, so when reindeer were introduced into Alaska at the turn of the twentieth century, on to pristine islands where there had been no previous grazing, this resulted in heavier animals developing there compared with those in Eurasia. Also it is a well-known fact that the process of domestication can produce a smaller animal than the wild equivalent. Thus domesticated reindeer are not only smaller than caribou but also smaller than wild reindeer in Eurasia.

A Striking Feature – the Antlers

One striking – quite literally – and common feature that links all but one of the members of the deer family is the presence of antlers. Antlers are a bit of a conundrum to many people because they fall off every year like a leaf on a tree and then re-grow. This annual process seems like rather a waste of energy, especially as there are only a few months in which the deer can grow them. Growth rate among deer with the largest antlers is very fast indeed, and in fact growing antler is thought to be the fastest-growing living tissue in the animal kingdom today.

It is perhaps useful at this stage to differentiate between antlers and horns, both appendages that grow out of the skull. Antlers are made of bone, whereas horn is made from a material called keratin – the same material as human fingernails. Like our fingernails, horn grows continuously from the base, so, for example, sheep, goats and antelope continually grow horns throughout their life. The blood supply at the base of the horn feeds the growing tissue which pushes outwards, thus extending the length of the constantly growing horn. The process of antler growth, however, is

Stripping velvet – with the blood supply cut off at the base the dead velvet strips away from the bony antlers in preparation for fighting.

completely different. The antler grows from a permanent protrusion from the skull called the pedicle, and is encased in a protective skin called velvet. The velvet actually carries blood vessels to the tip of the antler where it grows. In effect the antlers grow by a process of elongation. During the period of growth, when bone tissue is formed and ossifies, the antlers are covered in this protective velvet skin. However, once the antlers have grown to their full size then the blood supply at the base of the antlers is cut off and the velvet skin literally dies and peels away to reveal the hard bone antlers beneath. Once the velvet has gone the antlers cannot re-grow unless the hard bone antlers fall off and new velvet buds grow from the same place on the skull. Bone is a relatively brittle material compared with horn. Both appendages are mainly used as weapons for fighting but where horn is very durable and flexible, antlers are relatively easily broken. By casting their antlers and re-growing them the following year, deer can replace any broken antlers and an increase in size, related to age, can be achieved.

A Unique Feature

Among the majority of members of the deer family it is only the males that grow antlers because they use them to fight with other males to claim breeding females. Reindeer and caribou, however, are an exception to this rule because not only do the bulls grow antlers but so too do the cows and calves. In the case of the bulls their antlers are indeed there to fight with during the breeding season or rut. The bigger the antlers, and the larger the body, the more likely it is that a bull will win his contest and claim the cows.

However, it begs the question why do cow reindeer and indeed calves, regardless of sex, grow antlers too? The answer appears to lie in competition for food in winter time. The scarcity of vegetation during the arctic winter means that food is at a premium and the smaller female reindeer and calves need antlers to put them on a level playing field when competing for food with the larger males. In fact, after the rutting season and as the winter progresses, the oldest, most mature bulls are the first to cast their antlers. The presence of antlers greatly helps in terms of dominance and once they have fallen off the bull rapidly descends the pecking order. Those reindeer that have already lost their antlers, regardless of size, age or sex, will be bullied by those with antlers. As the winter goes by the younger bulls also cast their antlers to make way for the new ones to grow, but it is not until the females calve in spring that they too lose theirs. This means that as the winter goes on the cows become more and more dominant and move up the social pecking order. Many of these cows will of course be pregnant and gaining food is of paramount importance to their well-being and that of their calves. It would seem though that Rudolph and his male friends are at a great disadvantage in the winter by being antlerless. Certainly, if they kept them they wouldn't get bossed around by the girls. However, by losing their antlers first, and allowing pregnant cows to compete successfully for food, the mature bulls increase the chances of their offspring being born the following spring.

The size and complexity of antlers vary markedly between bulls and cows, with bull reindeer growing considerably bigger antlers than the cows, in terms of both weight and height. The males invest more heavily in antler growth, so that the male's antlers make up a higher proportion of total body weight compared with the female. As a secondary sexual characteristic, the size and complexity of a male's antlers, both for fighting and displaying with, are a heavy cost of successful reproduction. Confusion can arise between similar-sized antlers on a young bull and a mature cow but after casting there is an easy way to identify which are female antlers and which are male. The

Sorry Sirkas. From being number one breeding bull Sirkas has now cast his antlers and is at the bottom of the pack order, hence his downcast appearance.

difference is found at the point of casting, where the antler is joined to the pedicle. When cast, the base of the bull reindeer's antlers are convex or protruding, as if a small amount of the pedicle has come away with the antler, so leaving literally a hole in the head. In contrast, the base of the cow's antlers is concave or dished. This is a very important tool in helping to establish the sex ratio in populations of prehistoric reindeer at archaeological sites.

The size of a deer's antlers relative to body size tends to be related to the sociability of the species. Muntjac deer, which live in pairs, have short, simple antlers that emerge from very long, well-developed pedicles. The highly gregarious reindeer and caribou grow the largest and heaviest antlers in relation to body mass and the most complex and shapely antlers from small, almost non-existent pedicles. The antlers of a mature bull typically have a single wide 'spade-like' tine that grows forward across the front of the face. The main beam of the antler is long, and from it can grow many branching tines. Reindeer are the most evolutionarily advanced members of the deer family in terms of antler complexity.

Body Form and Shape

Textbook descriptions of reindeer tend to include words such as 'ungainly', 'thick muzzled' and 'flat-footed'. Certainly reindeer do not carry themselves as elegantly as many of the other deer species. In the *Monarch of the Glen*, the Victorian artist Sir Edwin Landseer accurately portrayed the red deer as an animal that holds its head high and is regal in its posture. In contrast, reindeer generally hold their heads low to the ground and only raise them when alarmed or fleeing from danger. Most deer species are slender in their build, light-footed and agile, while reindeer are much stockier, with strong, thick, powerful legs and an ability to travel across ground very economically. They are not in the habit of jumping unless they have to and then they do so with little style. The reindeer's winter coat is probably among the thickest and densest of any animal, enabling them to survive in the most demanding of arctic conditions. The thickness of coat, of course, only adds to the stocky appearance.

Rudolph's Relations

Until relatively recently reindeer and caribou were thought to be represented by a number of different species. However, after extensive work on reindeer genetics A.W.F. Banfield, an expert in the field of taxonomy (animal classification), concluded that all reindeer and caribou belong to the single species *Rangifer tarandus* and any apparent differences today are due to the geographical isolation of certain herds and the environmental conditions under which they live. This has resulted in nine sub-species, two of which, from east Greenland and Queen Charlotte Island, became extinct within the last hundred years. Fossil evidence has not been able to prove the origins of the genus Rangifer but most palaeontologists are agreed that reindeer and caribou originally came from Alaska, Beringia (a land bridge across the Bering Straits) or the mountains of north-east Asia. Today's caribou and reindeer are thought to have evolved from three geographically separated forms that survived in isolation from each other during the last glaciation.

Antler shape has been used to split the genus Rangifer into two main groups. The group Cylindricornis have antler beams which are round in cross-section and they occur in tundra and mountain environments. The second group, Compressicornis, have flattened antler beams and are generally found in forests and woodlands.

Cylindricornis

The group Cylindricornis were thought to originate in Beringia, which was once a land bridge between Siberia and

Forest reindeer and caribou, depicted here on the right, grow much flatter antlers than the tundra variety, seen on the left, thus splitting the genus into two main groups, Cylindricornis and Compressicornis.

Alaska. Today this group is split into a continental form, which is to be found in arctic tundra and higher latitudes of the great northern boreal forests of North America and Eurasia, and a high arctic form which is today restricted to the high arctic islands of Spitzbergen and Queen Elizabeth Islands.

Continental Reindeer

Briefly, the continental form in general undertake extensive migrations and their calves are born on the tundra during or at the end of the spring migration. The continental subspecies are represented by the Barren Ground Caribou, the Alaskan Caribou and the Eurasian Tundra Reindeer.

The **Barren Ground Caribou (R.t.groenlandicus)** is famous for the annual migration of massive herds from winter in the forest to distinct calving grounds on the tundra. This is what many people would regard as the typical caribou. Population numbers of large herds like this are difficult to estimate, but the total number of Barren Ground Caribou, split between a number of different herds in North America depending on the location of their calving grounds, is anything between 1.5 and 2 million animals. Their status is relatively secure in terms of sheer numbers but certain herds have had their grazing areas restricted by industrial development and their traditional migration routes have been interrupted by enormous pipelines servicing the exploitation of oil and gas in the North American arctic.

The Alaskan Caribou (*R.t.granti*), as its name suggests, is to be found in Alaska. The habits of this sub-species vary widely. Some live in forests in small groups, others in vast herds that migrate long distances to the tundra each year. Radio collars attached to female Alaskan Caribou have shown that they are capable of travelling 5,000km in one year, making them the most travelled land animal in the world. One of the best-known herds of Alaskan Caribou is the Western Arctic herd, whose numbers are estimated at around 500,000. They are a migrating herd with their calving grounds in the far north-west of Alaska. The Porcupine herd is another migrating herd of Alaskan reindeer that numbers approximately 150,000. Their summer grazing borders the Arctic Ocean on the north coast of Alaska.

The **Eurasian Tundra Reindeer (*R.t.tarandus*)** includes all reindeer, both wild and domesticated, to be found west of the Bering Straits, in the tundra and taiga zone of northern Russia and Scandinavia. Domesticated reindeer far outnumber wild reindeer, which today are confined to areas of Russia only, although there is an isolated population of wild reindeer (some experts believe they are not truly wild but feral) in the Hardangervidda in south Norway. By far the largest wild herd of reindeer in Russia is to be found in the Taimyr peninsula, where the total is about 600,000. There are at least another four wild herds which declined considerably during the first half of the twentieth century as a result of over-hunting and competition from domestic herds. However, a resurgence of

Bull caribou, North West Territory, Canada. Long slender legs and a lean body reflect the caribou's ability to migrate many thousands of miles in one year and run faster than its main predator the wolf.

numbers was experienced in recent years, partly as a result of fewer domestic reindeer as people became more centralised and left the nomadic way of life to live in towns. Even so their numbers are thought to total no more than 200,000. Like the continental caribou of North America, these reindeer are migratory, calving on the north coast of Russia and travelling south into the forested areas for the winter months.

High-arctic Reindeer

The high-arctic forms reindeer evolved in tundra regions north of the continental ice sheets in glacial refugia which are today represented by two island-living sub-species.

The **Svalbard Reindeer (*R.t.platrhynchus*)** is the smallest of all reindeer with a distinctive short face, short legs and a long, thick winter coat. Geographically isolated on the high

Short-legged, pot-bellied Svalbard Reindeer who remain sedentary in the high-arctic islands of Spitzbergen all year. An absence of predators means that they do not need to be able to run fast.

arctic islands of Svalbard for some 20,000 years, today's population numbers about 10,000. These reindeer live in the most nutritionally demanding conditions and experience great fluctuations in climate throughout the year. They do not undergo any form of migration. Over-hunting by man during the twentieth century undoubtedly led to an uncertain future for the Svalbard Reindeer. However, when the Norwegians took over the ownership of Svalbard they implemented a ban on hunting in 1925. This has secured the population for the foreseeable future.

The **Peary Caribou (*R.t.pearyi*)** is also small, though with longer legs than the Svalbard Reindeer. They are restricted to the high arctic Queen Elizabeth Islands of arctic Canada. In the summer of 1961 an estimate of 25,845 Peary Caribou was considered to be realistic but their numbers have dropped dramatically since then. Their future is unclear, after a significant decrease in population over recent years. On Banks Island the population dropped from 12,000 to 800 over a period of twenty years between the 1970s and 1990s. This drop has been attributed to many factors, including competition for grazing with another high arctic mammal, the musk ox, predation, hunting and severe weather conditions. The Canadian government has now added the Peary Caribou to its list of endangered animals and is actively trying to prevent the extinction of this sub-species.

Compressicornis

The woodland or forest form, Compressicornis, survived during the last glacial period in temperate refuges south of the continental ice sheet. This form is represented by the Eurasian Forest Reindeer and the North American Woodland Caribou. As a rule, this form is relatively sedentary, undergoing short altitudinal migrations between the seasons.

The **Eurasian Forest Reindeer (*R.t.fennicus*)** has a tremendous distribution throughout Russia, from Karelen in the west to the northern part of Sakhalin and southern Kamchatka in the east. They are mainly to be found in the Russian taiga zone, with some populations inhabiting the forests and mountainous areas of southern Siberia and north Mongolia. Because of the depth of snow in these forests during the winter these reindeer in general have the longest legs and biggest feet. Because of the diversity of habitats through the area the Eurasian Forest Reindeer can be found in a variety of types. The largest reindeer in Russia are a woodland sub-species from Kamchatka in the far eastern portion of Siberia at the coast of Okhotsk. These large-bodied reindeer form three distinct herds, two of which have dwindled in number and may even have disappeared. One herd has some protection in the Kronotsky Nature Reserve. Over-hunting has restricted its range to within the reserve.

In mountainous areas the woodland reindeer make short altitudinal migrations up into the mountains for summer

The information shown here has been collated from a number of sources and gives an approximate distribution of the different sub-species.

120°

RUSSIAN FEDERATION

pitzbergen

FINLAND

SWEDEN

90°E

60°

30°

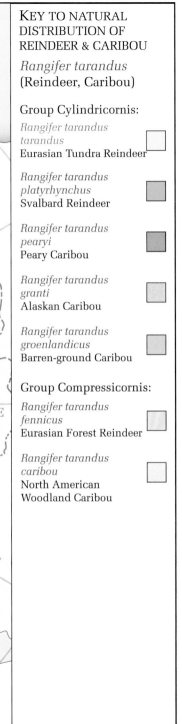

KEY TO NATURAL
DISTRIBUTION OF
REINDEER & CARIBOU

Rangifer tarandus
(Reindeer, Caribou)

Group Cylindricornis:

*Rangifer tarandus
tarandus*
Eurasian Tundra Reindeer

*Rangifer tarandus
platyrhynchus*
Svalbard Reindeer

*Rangifer tarandus
pearyi*
Peary Caribou

*Rangifer tarandus
granti*
Alaskan Caribou

*Rangifer tarandus
groenlandicus*
Barren-ground Caribou

Group Compressicornis:

*Rangifer tarandus
fennicus*
Eurasian Forest Reindeer

*Rangifer tarandus
caribou*
North American
Woodland Caribou

grazing and relief from heat and insects. The total number of wild forest reindeer in the taiga is difficult to estimate but is likely to be in the region of 60,000 and declining. Like the tundra reindeer, there is also a domesticated form of woodland reindeer.

The **North American Woodland Caribou (*R.t.caribou*)** is to be found from British Columbia to Newfoundland. This sub-species tends to live close to or in the boreal forest the whole year round, moves around in small groups and does not undertake vast seasonal movements typical of the tundra caribou. Sometimes known as 'the grey ghosts of the forest', woodland caribou can be very secretive and difficult to find. They generally live in small scattered groups moving continuously through the forested areas. They are extremely shy.

Within this sub-species, however, there are also the mountain caribou, which, by nature of their environment, make short annual excursions up into the mountains for the summer and travel back into the forest for the winter. Their migrations are never usually longer than 50km, with an elevation change of 300m. These are some of the largest caribou in the world in terms of body size and antlers.

Because of the nature of their habits it is difficult to put a number on the total population of Woodland Caribou. Sadly they are particularly vulnerable to logging activities and large areas clear-felled for the timber industry have destroyed important grazing areas. The population is decreasing and may be in the region of 750,000.

One must be wary, however, of names that seemingly describe the habits of a particular group of reindeer, because the sub-species designations, arrived at as a result of the study of their ancestry, may not always relate to the current ecological conditions that they live in. Indeed, there are numerous examples where populations of the same sub-species have evolved different adaptations in response to environmental conditions. The caribou of the George River herd in Quebec, for example, which belong to the Woodland Caribou sub-species, actually represent the largest caribou herd in the world, migrating thousands of miles from boreal forest to open tundra where most of the cows calve together in a space of just three weeks. This type of behaviour is much more typical of the Barren Ground Caribou sub-species. Since taxonomic designations can be confusing, it is sometimes better simply to look at the environment of a population of caribou or reindeer, rather than getting too involved in their evolutionary origins.

Extinctions

Within the last hundred years two sub-species of caribou have become extinct, the **East Greenland caribou (*R.t.eogroenlandicus*)** and the **Queen Charlotte Island Caribou (*R.t.dawsoni*)**. The extinction of the East Greenland Caribou in the early 1900s was probably associated with natural climate change which led to an absence of sea-ice and the heavy accumulation of snow in winter. This meant that these caribou were unable to move across the sea-ice to other islands to graze and so the population died out. A similar decline was seen in other mainland caribou herds at the time but they subsequently recovered.

The Queen Charlotte Island Caribou struggled on until 1935, when they too were thought to become extinct. There is no evidence to suggest that their demise was directly related to human activities and the common view is that these two sub-species were evolutionarily senile and became extinct through natural causes.

The Reindeer Year

The life cycle of reindeer and caribou is closely entwined with the changing seasons and can be succinctly summed up as spring calving, summer growing, autumn mating and winter surviving. The arctic summer is short but intense and the winters are long and arduous. Depending on outside factors such as predation, insect harassment and sources of vegetation, herds of caribou and wild reindeer react differently to achieve the same ultimate aim – to find enough food to grow and reproduce while at the same time avoiding being eaten by something else.

Spring

Spring is the time when reindeer and caribou must find a place to calve. Often they return to traditional calving grounds, which may be close to the winter range or many hundreds of miles away. The urge to move and the distance to go are determined by the desire for good grazing and the need to find a safe haven from wolves, by far the most important predators of caribou because of their size, speed of reproduction and method of killing. The wolf is a dedicated predator, unlike the bear, which is an omnivore and by choice will turn vegetarian at various times of year and then hibernate for six months. Various sub-species of timber and tundra wolves have a holarctic distribution which mirrors that of caribou and the wolves' behaviour has a great influence on the way the caribou behave.

Female Barren Ground Caribou have to travel as far as 600 miles to their preferred calving grounds on the tundra, close to the Arctic Ocean. April sees a stirring in the herd which, depending on snow conditions and the fitness of the caribou, will see the cows travelling anything up to 30 miles a day to reach the calving grounds before their young are born. Their migration will involve sometimes thousands of animals taking unpredictable routes. If they are lucky they may cross windswept ridges and frozen lakes, but if not they may also encounter barriers like deep canyons and rivers in spate. While they are competent swimmers and efficient travellers across snow, the weather conditions may sometimes halt or divert their progress and they must wait or change direction. Although spring is already taking over in their winter ranges, the cows must face difficult wintry conditions at the calving grounds. At least the concerted effort has taken them far from the majority of the wolves, who are left behind to den in the forest margin, and the strenuous move is completed before they give birth to small and vulnerable calves that would have slowed their progress. As well as reducing the pressure of wolf predation, migration to these calving grounds next to the Arctic Ocean also delays the onset of biting insects which can be a particular torment for the young calves with their short coats and thin sensitive skin.

The strategies adopted by different herds of reindeer when they calve depend on different factors. Large aggregations of breeding females at traditional sites are well known, but sedentary woodland populations pursue a more secretive approach. The females disperse at calving time and remain alone with their new calf throughout much of the spring and summer. Fewer in number than the tundra caribou, their strategy of spreading themselves out thinly throughout the boreal forest in the summer and keeping on the move makes it more difficult for the predators to find them.

Calving

Caribou cows are generally sexually mature at 1½ years old and so will have their first calf when they are 2 years old. Sexual maturity, however, is determined by achieving a certain body weight and if this is reached when they are 6 months old then cows will calve at a year old. Following a seven-and-a-half-month gestation a single calf is normally born and the quantity of milk that each calf receives is small, normally no more than ⅓ litre per day. The cow's udder is small and compact and almost completely concealed in hair to conserve heat and prevent frostbite. There would be no advantage for a caribou living in sub-zero conditions to have an udder like a Jersey cow. (The calf would be living off ice-cream!)

Although low in quantity, caribou milk is rich in fat, protein and vitamins, and contains a considerable amount of dry matter. The lactation period is from calving in April or May until the calf self-weans in September or October. During that six-month period the calf will receive no more than 40 to 45 litres of milk. The calves are completely dependent on their mothers' milk at birth and during their first few weeks they obtain all their nutritional requirements from her until their stomachs have developed enough to properly ruminate vegetation. The quality of the mother's milk is closely related to the quality of food that the cow can find, and so the green shoots of the spring vegetation are extremely important to the early development of the calf.

Caribou are one of the few deer species whose calves are unspotted at birth. They do not resemble the typical 'Bambi' at all, as their normal coat colour is chestnut brown with a black back. Camouflage is vitally important for a vulnerable calf and the combination of colours blends perfectly into the background of bare ground and patches of snow. Calving can occur in difficult weather, including snow, severe frost or cold rain, but the calves have an extremely well-insulated coat to cope with this.

Weighing anything up to 7kg at birth, the calves are very precocious. They are able to stand soon after birth and within hours can run with their mothers. The strategy adopted by caribou is for the calf to flee from danger with its mother rather than hide in the undergrowth like many of the other deer species. This is a response to their environment, which is often open, with few hiding places, and to the fact that their main predator, the wolf, is very mobile. Mother/calf recognition is most consistently achieved by smell and sound. The individual grunts of a calf get the mother to grunt back and on contact she will smell the calf to double-check.

In the early weeks of life the calf stays close to her mother, the lush carpet of vegetation providing all the nutritional requirements for rich milk production and growth.

As a general rule, the pregnant cows keep their old bony antlers until they calve, and then cast these antlers to make way for the new velvet antlers to grow. Indeed, it is quite often the case that the new velvet antlers push off the old ones. The demand for calcium is at its peak during this phase of milk production and antler growth, and in calcium-depleted areas the discarded antlers do not go to waste. In one of the best examples of recycling in the animal kingdom, the reindeer chew their antlers to replenish their calcium reserves, which will be required over the summer months.

Bulls

In contrast to the cows, the bulls of migrating caribou herds think only of their stomachs and instead of following the cows north they stay in the winter range to run the gauntlet of predators. By lagging behind the cows the bulls get the full benefit of the spring growth of vegetation in the more southerly areas. The food is more abundant and nutritious here but they constantly run the risk of being eaten by Mr Wolf. However, the combination of good food and repeatedly running away from the wolves provides a good workout for a potential breeding bull the following autumn.

But the urge to move north to where the cows are eventually prevails. By doing so, they move with the advancing spring, so benefiting from the best growth of vegetation.

Still in full winter coat and with just three months' growth of antler, this reindeer bull already has an impressive set of velvet antlers.

Summer

As summer progresses, the bulls and cows of migrating herds gather in massive groups and move rapidly and erratically across the tundra driven by biting insects, in particular mosquitoes. The female mosquito needs blood to lay viable eggs and so focuses on the areas that are less hairy or have thinner skin. The newly growing velvet antlers are particularly vulnerable and on warm sunny days these insects can make life pretty miserable for a caribou. By forming large groups the caribou try to reduce the level of harassment, presumably by passing the problem on to their neighbours. Coastal breezes and permanent snowfields both help to ease the effect but the insects are savage and the caribou find themselves in a catch-22 situation, where food is abundant but the insects prevent efficient feeding. Luckily though, their summer range is the land of the midnight sun, which means 24 hours of daylight and thus 24 hours growth of vegetation and potential grazing. The constant daylight is the saving grace of the tundra, producing a profusion of growth of both animal and plant life. During the cooler hours of the day the insects are less active and the caribou can catch up on lost grazing time.

It is imperative that the calf grows quickly from birth. Nutritious reindeer milk and good summer grazing means that a calf can double its birthweight in two to three weeks, and with a daily weight gain of between 300g and 550g reindeer calves may weigh as much as 50kg by the autumn. In addition to this rapid growth, and laying down body reserves for the winter, the calves also have to grow their first set of antlers, moult their calf coat and grow their first summer coat, followed in quick succession by the onset of growing their thick insulating winter coat. This all has to happen in a comparatively short space of time during the summer and autumn to ensure survival through the winter months.

In its first few weeks of life the calf is never far from its mother's side, lying close to where she browses and always following on when she moves on to fresh ground. As the calf grows older it becomes more adventurous, leaving its mother's side and spending more time with the other calves. Forming 'nurseries', the calves enjoy one another's company and often become playful in the twilight hours. From small protrusions on its head, the first set of antlers begins to grow when the calf is around a month old. Over the next few months the antlers will grow in order to enable the calf to compete for food in the winter months. The size of the calves' antlers by the end of the summer will vary greatly depending on the quality of their diet. A fully grown set of calf antlers may be as long as 40cm with a couple of points.

As the summer progresses the calf coat is moulted to reveal their first adult summer coat. This coincides with the adults moulting their old winter coat. The thick, light-coloured winter coat falls away to reveal a short dark summer coat underneath. Caribou and reindeer can look decidedly moth-eaten at this stage. Like many other arctic animals, they undergo a coat colour change between winter and summer, from light to dark. By the end of July they are all in full summer coat; combined with their newly grown velvet antlers, this makes the reindeer look very sleek.

With moulting complete, the short, dark summer coat and long velvet antlers give reindeer the 'elegant look'.

Adults also have to make the most of the rich summer grazing by laying down fat reserves for the winter. The quality of summer grazing is vitally important for this and also to ensure a fast rate of antler growth, particularly among the bulls who need to be ready for the rutting season.

Autumn

With the first snaps of frost in late August the insect numbers decline and finding food takes priority. The food is still abundant and provides enough energy to continue antler and body growth and to build up fat reserves. The reindeer are now really looking their best. Already the new winter coat is beginning to grow in, the thicker, paler coat contrasting with the dark summer coat. With their antlers fully grown, the blood supply at the base is cut off and the velvet literally peels away. Thrashing the antlers against vegetation helps to speed up the process but is not essential as the velvet skin is dead and will just fall off anyway. Underneath are revealed the hard bone antlers which can often look decidedly bloody for a couple of days. The bulls are the first to strip the velvet in preparation for the rutting season. They are followed by the cows and calves a few weeks later.

With a gestation period of seven and a half months conception needs to take place in the autumn to ensure the calves are born in spring. The rutting season is a time of strenuous activity for the bulls, which have spent the summer preparing themselves. The reproductive strategy in reindeer is for one bull to claim a harem of cows. As well as chasing other prospective bulls away the bull must constantly gather his wandering females and of course copulate with any female that is receptive. The breeding bulls are so busy they have not the time or inclination to eat and so rapidly lose weight. This creates a potentially dangerous situation as they then have to face the rigours of the winter in poor shape. Indeed there can be substantial mortality among the breeding bulls during the winter months, which is a contributory factor in average life expectancy. Bull caribou and reindeer tend to have a shorter life expectancy than the cows.

Bulls fighting. With antlers locked together this trial of strength results in the winner claiming the number one spot and the harem of breeding cows.

Caribou bulls normally breed for the first time at 3 or 4 years old and will usually reach their prime at about 6 years old. The contest between reindeer bulls entails both an element of display and a show of strength, although a degree of experience will also stand a bull in good stead. During the weeks leading up to the rut the neck muscles of a breeding bull swell and this combines with increased bodyweight to form the powerhouse with which they will do battle. The antlers, now stripped of their velvet, act both as ornaments to display with and as handles to lock the heads of two bulls together for a pushing match. Displaying between two bulls often involves parallel walking, where two bulls will walk side by side eyeing each other up. In some instances the sheer size of a bull's antlers is enough to deter a prospective challenger. However, if the display alone is insufficient, a fight will commence. The bulls lock antlers and push. During this battle of strength they may break their antler lock and re-engage a number of times, turning on a sixpence before clashing heads again. Battles may last for some time. Although injuries do occur, the outcome is seldom fatal. The winner of any contest will drive the loser away and will remain dominant over his opponent until such time as he tires, breaks his antlers or becomes injured.

Winter

For migrating reindeer and caribou the general trend is to move back towards the forests for the winter to escape the severe weather on the tundra. But in many respects it is out of the frying pan and into the fire because they are now back in wolf territory and the pressure is on once again from predation. When the caribou are unavailable in summer the wolves basically starve. A diet of fish, small mammals and birds is not sufficient to support adults and raise pups, and so when the caribou return for the winter the wolves are literally ravenous and desperate for a good meal. Any nutritional stress that wolf pups endure over the summer ends in September with the return of the caribou. So the wolf makes the most of the migrating caribou by staying in the tree line. In this way he can feed off the winter population, the spring population of lingering bulls and the autumn population of returning herds for the winter.

Over the winter the caribou have an unpredictable lifestyle, moving erratically and in no particular direction in a bid to find sufficient food to sustain themselves and outwit the predators, in particular wolf and man. Certainly the frustration of hunters trying to locate caribou in the winter is well known and is perhaps best summed up by a North American Indian proverb, 'Nobody knows of the wind or the Caribou'. Winter is a time of sheer survival. But reindeer and caribou are perfectly adapted to survive the arduous weather conditions and the resulting deprivation of food.

FOUR

Hairy Bums, Flat Feet and Velvet Noses

It is the middle of winter, pitch dark and −20 °C, and as I step out of the aeroplane at Lapland Airport in north Sweden I am immediately appreciative of the need for reindeer living at these latitudes to be able to cope with the cold. It is *freezing*. As I exhale, my warm breath freezes on my cold chin. Despite many layers of clothing and thick socks, there is no way I am going to stay out in this for long. Luckily, our hire car is there ready for us to jump into, plugged into mains electricity to prevent it freezing solid. This is no place for a soft southerner, but reindeer and caribou are totally 'at home' in this harsh environment.

Full Body Cover and Tog Factor 15+

From the tips of their noses to the soles of their feet, reindeer are covered in hair (indeed, the only bare bit is their eyeballs and there is a very good reason for this, to do with vision!). In addition, the quality and density of a reindeer's coat are unsurpassed. The coat is made up of two types of hair. Hollow guard hairs, which are composed of a matrix of air-filled cells, are anything up to 4 or 5cm long and densely packed at approximately 670 per sq. cm. The hair root itself is thin but outside the skin the guard hair expands immensely. Below this is a fine woolly coat, not air-filled but much denser at approximately 2,000 per sq. cm. The combination of the two types allows the good heat-insulating capacity of the reindeer's coat. In fact their coat can be likened to an extremely high tog-

Reindeer are so well insulated that they
don't even melt the snow they lie on.

value duvet filled with hollow
fill, air of course being one of
the best forms of insulation. By
inhibiting loss of heat through
radiation, reindeer can lie on
snow without melting it and so
a layer of snow on the ground
provides a comfortable dry bed
for a reindeer. Also snow that
lands on their backs remains
unmelted and can itself add to
the insulation value. A reindeer
is like an enormous thermos
flask wandering around, its
coat letting no heat out and no
cold in. Indeed, reindeer skin
with the hair on is the warmest
clothing you could ask for, even for your feet. Reindeer-skin
boots were the only footwear that kept my feet warm in
Lapland. With no hard sole, just skin, I felt as though I was
walking about on the snow with my slippers on, but in this dry,
cold environment reindeer-skin boots were the business.

Like the adults, the calves too have a very high-quality coat
when they are born. They lack the hollow guard hairs but
make up for that with a very dense soft coat of 3,200 hairs per
sq. cm. Thermal quality remains high as long as the conditions
are dry. However, water greatly reduces the warmth of the
calf's coat and if very wet conditions prevail during the
calving season then high mortality can be experienced.

Svalbard Reindeer, the most northerly plant-eating mammal,
have a particularly superior coat to be able to cope with the
high-arctic island weather conditions. Although only 30 per
cent thicker than that of mainland reindeer, it has
approximately twice the insulation value. Calves on Svalbard
generally enjoy a much higher survival rate despite the extreme
fluctuations in the weather conditions, and many scientists feel
this is to a large extent due to the very high coat quality.

One of the most endearing features of reindeer are their soft velvet noses. As well as protecting them against frost bite, it makes them a delight to hand feed.

In all reindeer the facial hair extends down to their lips. This is an extremely important requirement in sub-arctic conditions and no doubt hardened polar explorers grow beards for the same reason. Breathing out warm air into sub-zero conditions creates a build-up of frost on any cold wet surface, like lips. By having a completely hairy muzzle reindeer avoid this and instead can go about their everyday business with warm, dry noses. That warm, dry nose has to be thrust down through the snow to find food in winter, so their velvet nose is also an important asset when it comes to winter feeding.

Overheating

Of course there is a downside to having such a well-insulated coat. First, the reindeer can become rather hot when the season changes and the climate warms. And if they have to exert themselves, perhaps by sprinting away from a predator, then overheating can be a problem. Their thick coat reduces heat loss from the body by radiation, and the skin of a reindeer has no sweat glands to help them lose heat. Reindeer do go through a spring moult where the longer guard hairs fall out, exposing the darker undercoat beneath. This is a help, but even so for reindeer to lose heat effectively they have to hyperventilate or pant like a dog. Heat is then dissipated from the highly vascular tongue and through expelling hot air. In the spring and summer their newly growing velvet antlers are also very vascular, with the blood vessels close to the skin. In effect they work as radiators, and it has been suggested that the reason for reindeer growing antlers is actually to radiate heat in the summer time, thus explaining why cows and calves also grow antlers.

Vulnerable Extremities

Compared with other species of deer, reindeer are more heavily built and stockier. By having a low body-to-surface area ratio reindeer lose relatively less heat. And the Svalbard reindeer are the dumpiest of all because a compact shape lends itself better to saving energy. Because Svalbard reindeer are basically sedentary, owing to the lack of predation and their restricted grazing range, they have relatively short, fat legs, which also help to combat the cold.

Caribou and reindeer living on the mainland have much longer, thinner legs than high-arctic reindeer. This enables them both to travel efficiently and flee from predators effectively but it does mean that their legs are more vulnerable to heat loss. However, a specialised arrangement of blood vessels going to and from the legs counters this problem. Warm blood flowing to the legs passes closely by the cold blood returning from the legs. This allows some heat exchange between the two and the warm blood going to the legs is cooled by the cool blood leaving the legs. The overall effect is that there is very little heat loss from the legs.

A similar heat-exchange system operates in the nasal passages of the reindeer. They have particularly complicated nostrils with bone and cartilage designed like a 'rolled scroll'. This, combined with many fine, short hairs, creates a highly effective method of retaining heat and water. By greatly increasing the surface area of the nostrils, blood can warm the cold incoming air. This enables the water in the air to condense and it then trickles back into special folds, which direct it to the back of the nose and into the throat. This nasal heat exchange protects the reindeer from heat and water loss during respiration in the cold.

Reindeer ears are relatively short compared with other species of deer and are covered mostly in stiff hairs to trap air, ensuring that frostbite does not affect the thinnest parts of the body.

Flat Feet

Compared with all the other species of deer, reindeer and caribou have relatively large feet for the size of their bodies. Their hooves are concave with sharp edges and their dew claws are also large. Both the back dew claws and the main cloven hooves can be spread far apart. Splayed hooves spread the weight of the reindeer across a larger surface area, and so the weight load on the ground from individual feet is low. Studies comparing reindeer with moose reveal that the weight load of each foot of a reindeer is four times less than that of a moose. On their travels reindeer regularly encounter soft, deep snow and wet, boggy ground at different times of year, so spreading their weight to allow them to travel with little effort is vitally important.

When travelling through snow reindeer invariably follow one another's tracks to save energy. Moreover their back feet are placed in the prints of the front feet, so lessening the tendency for all four feet to sink into the snow, the front foot having already compacted the surface for the back foot. Their dished hooves also make very effective shovels. They can break through crusted snow and thin ice as well as dig down through up to a metre of snow to find food below. They have a good sense of smell and never dig in vain.

Once the snow melts, the rivers rise and the lakes get flooded. To negotiate these natural barriers reindeer need to be good swimmers. Their large feet act as effective paddles

Snow trail of reindeer. In deep snow reindeer save energy by
following each other's tracks.

while their air-filled coat gives them buoyancy, enabling them
to tackle rivers in spate, flooded lakes and even Norwegian
fjords to reach outlying islands for summer grazing.

Silent but Clicking

During the winter months reindeer and caribou are virtually
silent. In the spring a cow and her new-born calf will grunt

to each other, while in the autumn the bulls will grunt to warn off challengers. But grunting is costly, because by expelling air to grunt the animal loses heat. Thus grunting is kept to a minimum during the winter months. However, reindeer and caribou are extremely sociable animals and prefer to stay together. In low visibility, blizzard conditions or thick fog they can locate each other by clicking their tendons. As the reindeer articulates its foot a tendon in the joint above slips across the joint, producing a clicking noise. All reindeer and caribou click, and when a large number are on the move together the clicking is very loud. There is very little energy cost involved so the herd can remain in contact without losing valuable heat.

Winter Strategies

After the frenzy of eating in the summer reindeer show a decline in food consumption during the winter months. This reduced appetite, combined with a lower metabolic rate, means that long periods of the day can be spent lying up and resting, further increasing energy conservation. It is a very obvious behaviour of reindeer that they will happily remain motionless for relatively long periods of time during the winter. Patience is second nature to them.

Reindeer will eat snow in preference to drinking water. This is very sensible, bearing in mind the abundance of snow and the dearth of running water in the winter. The loss of body heat to melt snow for drinking water far outweighs the potential loss of body heat that would be incurred in searching for copious amounts of water.

Reindeer are past masters at reducing their nutritional and water demands in winter to conserve energy and survive. Reducing the frequency of urination also helps to achieve this. With a reduced intake of food there is less toxic waste to excrete, so less urination. And as snow is basically demineralised water, the excretion of minerals through urination is also kept to a minimum.

Feast and Famine

The most important factor for all life on earth is the light and heat radiated from the sun. Throughout the far north summer is a season of abundant light and winter a time of darkness, with solar radiation further compromised because the sun is very low in the sky during the winter months. Thus by the time the rays reach earth they have lost all their energy passing through the atmosphere. The reduced light intensity and low daytime temperatures for much of the year, combined with strong winds, high humidity, permafrost, extended snow cover and poor, shallow soils, scarce in nutrients, all influence the type of plants found in the far north.

In the far north the flora is characteristically short in stature with widely spreading root systems close to the surface. Many have developed ways to help them withstand the severe winters, often by existing in a latent vegetative state or by continuing to grow under the snow. Creeping plants, trailing thickets, cushioned leaves and dense turfs are common forms of vegetation, and there are some 800 species of vascular plants and 900 more primitive mosses and lichens to be found.

At least 90 per cent of arctic and alpine vascular plants are small perennials which grow slowly over a number of years. Many are succulents, able to store water in their fleshy leaves and stems. Other methods to prevent drying out include the growth of thick cuticles and a reduction in leaf size. Further adaptations to help them withstand heat and water loss include acquiring a cushion form to reduce surface area, a build-up of concentrated sap, which acts like antifreeze in a car radiator, and generating warmth by the fermenting of

Tundra vegetation. Rich summer grazing is the key to survival for reindeer in winter time.

sugars, releasing heat energy from the disintegrating molecules.

This arctic flora is found on the tundra, a treeless landscape along the coast of the Arctic Ocean. The word tundra originally derived from the Finnish word *tunturi*, meaning completely treeless heights. The mountain or alpine tundra endures similar climatic factors and has a corresponding ecology; it is especially widespread in much of the mountainous areas of Siberia and Alaska and develops at altitude above the upper tree line. A defining feature of tundra is the dominance of mosses, which form the basic building blocks of this windswept habitat, along with lichens. The flowering plants consist mainly of sedges, cotton grasses and other grasses, bushes such as willow, alder and birch, dwarf shrubs including heathers, bilberries, whortleberries and cowberries, and a few herbaceous perennials.

As latitude and altitude decrease, the treeless landscape gives way to scattered groups of stunted larch, spruce, birch and willow trees. This is the northerly edge of the great belt of coniferous forest known as the boreal or northern forest, which extends across Eurasia and North America. In the Arctic the winters are long and the summers short. Although the summers can be hotter further south, the winters can still see temperatures as low as −40 °C. Low rainfall and low temperatures, combined with poor soils, govern the region's plant life.

The coniferous forest extends some 8,000 miles and is only broken by the Atlantic and Pacific Oceans. Within its scope are the mountainous areas of the Urals in Eurasia and the Mackenzies in North America, which create a mountain habitat in the boreal forest. Massive rivers flow northwards out of these mountain ranges to the Arctic. Like the arctic tundra, the boreal forest or taiga habitat is a mosaic of standing water, lakes and swamps. Taiga is a Russian word meaning 'swamp forest'.

It is within this inhospitable and often harsh environment that the various sub-species of reindeer and caribou are to be found, adapting themselves to the immediate environmental conditions of their range whether it be the high-arctic islands of Svalbard or the boreal forest of Siberia.

Growth and Body Condition

As seasonal breeders, reindeer and caribou time the birth of their calves to coincide with the wealth of vegetation available in the summer months and by the following year male and female yearlings will have achieved nearly their full skeletal size. Already heavier than the females by this age, the males continue to grow and may well not achieve their maximum weight until they are 3 or 4 years old.

There are big differences between male and female reindeer and caribou when it comes to body size and weight; indeed, among all the deer species they show the most marked sexual dimorphism in this area. The acquisition of sufficient fat reserves is a critical factor for all animals living in a highly seasonal environment, and is closely related to the energetic requirements associated with reproduction.

Male reindeer and caribou attain their peak weight in late summer but lose condition rapidly during the rut in autumn. Then, already exhausted, they have to face the winter. Females do not reach their peak condition until late autumn. They then steadily lose condition over the winter months, declining to a minimum when they calve in spring. After calving and during early lactation the cows are in their poorest condition. However, the biggest weight change, and correspondingly greater demand on resources, is incurred by the males, who will lose up to twice as much of their body tissue as the females, in the form of fat and muscle, over the rut and winter months. The cost of reproduction is far higher for males and this contributes to their shorter average life span.

Summer Feast

The long summer days, climaxing in constant daylight at mid-summer, generate a profusion of rich vegetation, and it is this abundance that enables reindeer and caribou to thrive in the north. Over the summer months it is essential for them to lay down enough fat reserves to see them through the lean times in the winter. There will be many occasions when the snow is too deep or too hard to dig through and the reindeer will have to go without food of any sort. Sufficient body reserves are needed to bring them through these periods of starvation. Despite all their adaptations to survive the cold, without the profusion of growth in the arctic summer, reindeer and caribou would never be able to prepare themselves sufficiently for eight months of snow. They are supremely adapted for their winter environment – but they are equally well adapted to make the most of the summer's bounty.

Caribou and reindeer are described as mixed feeders, intermediate between roughage feeders and concentrate selectors, grazing fastidiously on fresh and untouched green vegetation. Some plants they consume completely, others only partially. They eat on the hoof, never staying in one place for long, and where they can they make the most of the advancing spring as they move north towards the Arctic Ocean or up into the high mountains. Reindeer and caribou pursue a selective feeding strategy, consuming large amounts of highly digestible forage which has a relatively rapid rate of passage through the digestive system.

The green plants contain all the nutrients and vitamins required for growth. Willow and birch shrubs are very valuable fodder, being high in protein and minerals. Leaves are plucked and eaten as soon as they appear, and continue to be consumed avidly through the whole of the summer. Consisting of at least 20 per cent protein, these leaves form the basis of reindeer growth. In some areas 80 per cent of the intake of food is made up of foliage. Sedges and cotton grasses are also rich in protein before they flower and are eagerly consumed in the spring when they are juicy and tender. Cotton grasses are extremely important in some areas, representing as much as 90 per cent of the summer food. The primitive horsetails are also enthusiastically eaten.

Herbaceous plants are often the preferred food of reindeer and caribou. They are rich in nutrients, often with high concentrations of protein, carbohydrates and vitamins. They tend to develop later than grasses and sedges and are a very important component of the reindeers' diet in late summer before the first frosts turn them brown and unpalatable. Ladysmantle, marsh marigolds, cloudberry, lousewort, sorrel, bogbean and irises are all consumed during the summer months.

Reindeer and caribou are thought to eat more than 350 different species of plants during the summer months in their quest to prepare themselves for the imminent falls of snow, plummeting temperatures and frozen ground.

Magic Mushrooms

In certain areas the end of the summer also sees the fruiting bodies of mushrooms, which are a highly prized source of food for reindeer and caribou. Although mushrooms consist of over 90 per cent water, they are rich in proteins, have a high potassium and phosphorus content and contain numerous vitamins. The yield of mushrooms is promoted by warm, wet weather, and in the southerly zones of the tundra, where the taiga begins, many mushrooms grow. Reindeer can detect the scent of suitable mushrooms from some distance, and their scattered pattern of growth will cause the animals to move about erratically in late summer. Highly favoured are the boletus mushrooms, which are rich in nutrients and are eagerly devoured. In the forest margins the red boletus variety can reach a weight of 1.5kg.

Boletus mushroom, a great delicacy for reindeer but which also provides them with a rich food source before the onset of winter.

Winter Famine

While there is plenty of choice in the summer, winter offers an extremely limited menu. Reindeer and caribou have to resort to a much more impoverished diet, which for the vast majority means lichens. The relationship between reindeer and lichens has been long recognised and Carolus Linnaeus, one of the early taxonomists in the eighteenth century, called the lichen that reindeer ate *Lichen rangiferinas*, in recognition of their close relationship. Since then his *Lichen rangiferinas* has been reclassified into 200 different species belonging to various genera.

Lichens are very interesting. They actually consist of two different 'plants' in a symbiotic relationship. The main body, or thallus, is made up of a fungus, which grows like other fungi by living on a supply of organic food. Within the fungus live unicellular algae, which contain chlorophyll and grow by the process of photosynthesis. The fungal component and the algae all live on the food manufactured by the algae. The unicellular algae that invade the cells of the fungus are supported by the fungal threads.

Lichens are rootless, obtaining all of their water from either moisture in the air, dew or precipitation. A dry mat of lichen will absorb water from a shower of rain very readily, catching the water before it can even wet the soil below. Indeed, the water capacity of lichen is enormous, and they are able to absorb four or five times their own weight in water. On well-drained mineral soils in a climate where there is little precipitation, the lichens are able to compete very successfully with higher vascular plants, which can only obtain their water via roots in the soil. This also explains why lichens are able to grow in the absence of soil, on trees and rocks. Lichens are widespread throughout the world, and are found in some very remote and inhospitable places. Seven species of rock lichens, for example, are to be found close to the South Pole and also at altitudes of 18,000ft.

In some areas lichen will comprise as much as 80 per cent of the reindeers' total winter diet. The lichens generally preferred by reindeer and caribou are the mats of ground lichens, particularly fruticose lichens, including Alectoria, Cetraria,

Lichen, the staple diet for most populations of reindeer and caribou during the winter months. Full of carbohydrate but low in protein, it is a high-energy snack that enables them to survive the long winters.

Cladonia and Stereocaulon, which are found on dry and exposed hills and ridges of the arctic, sub-arctic and alpine landscape. These lichens also dominate on the easily drained soils between scattered trees in the boreal forest, where one also finds epiphytic or tree lichens. The latter are another source that can provide part of the reindeer and caribou's winter fare.

Lichens are very slow growing. Periods of accumulation of organic and inorganic substances, when growth can take place, alternate with periods of rest when no carbon dioxide is absorbed and growth ceases. During periods of snow cover the unicellular algae cease to photosynthesise owing to lack of light, and during very dry conditions the lichen goes into a resting state. Annual growth rates are no more than 50mm per year. This slow rate of regeneration makes lichen pastures very susceptible to overgrazing during the winter months, and because of their fragile nature they are also prone to the effects of trampling during dry periods in the summer. By moving away from the winter lichen pastures in the summer, and spreading out the winter grazing population over a large area, the reindeer and caribou protect their crucial supply of winter fodder.

Of the 16,000 species of lichen classified so far, reindeer and caribou only choose to eat about 50 different species. Poor in protein but rich in carbohydrate, lichens provide reindeer and caribou with instant energy but an overall negative nitrogen balance. In other words, reindeer survive but don't grow on the lichen diet, steadily losing condition over the winter. Although highly favoured by reindeer and caribou, lichen is not the only food they consume in the winter months. They must also search for remnants of green vegetation which are fully or partially preserved under the snow. These are most easily reached during the early winter period when the snow is still soft. The leaves and roots of horsetails, grasses and sedges, cotton grasses and woody shrubs are all eaten in varying proportions.

Lichen: Perfect but not Essential

Until relatively recently it was assumed that all reindeer and caribou populations depended on a lichen-based diet in the winter months. This niche was unoccupied by other northern species of deer and other herbivores, including musk ox and mountain sheep, even though their ranges overlap with those of the reindeer and caribou. Without a doubt the large splayed hooves of the reindeer and caribou have evolved as efficient digging tools to reach the lichen through the snow, so adapting them to this specialised diet.

However, research into high-arctic populations of reindeer and caribou has shown that lichen as a winter source of food was not essential, and the animals relied on other sources of food in these areas. Svalbard Reindeer, Peary Caribou and the Barren Ground Caribou of Greenland are all basically sedentary populations that live in the high arctic. Although they may make short altitudinal moves, or slightly longer inter-island journeys across the sea ice, they are basically non-migratory. The reindeer and caribou here have adapted to a life without lichen, instead feeding extensively on dead grasses and sedges during the winter months.

Carnivorous Herbivores

Snow, which is effectively distilled water with zero mineral content, protein-deficient lichens and meagre portions of dried grasses, sedges and other vascular plants from the previous summer make up the impoverished menu available to reindeer and caribou during the long, dark, winter months. This depleted diet causes cravings, which may include a lusting for salt and even the consumption of dead animals. There have been well-documented incidents of reindeer eating meat and fish discarded by man. As active hunters, they have been known to pursue and kill lemmings, and indeed lemming skins have been found in the stomachs of dead reindeer. The gnawing of bones is also quite common and, as in other species of deer, the antlers are chewed as a source of nutrition, particularly in regions of calcium-deficient soils, but reindeer also extend their dietary habits to eating bird droppings and animal and human urine. They have even been seen to chew on other dead reindeer. The phrase 'don't eat yellow snow' is not one reindeer would adhere to!

SIX

The Early Taming of Reindeer

Reindeer and the Ice Age

The earliest European fossils of reindeer were found in Sussenborn, Germany, and are estimated to be 440,000 years old. This date coincides with the start of the last Ice Age, which began about 500,000 years ago and finished about 10,000 years ago.

Known in geological terms as the Middle and Upper Pleistocene or the Quaternary period, it was considerably colder than it is today but only for relatively short periods of time when there were widespread glaciations and polar deserts across Eurasia and North America. South of the glaciers the cold, dry and relatively stable climatic conditions fostered an abundance of life characteristic of treeless 'steppe-tundra'. A rich profusion of grasses, sedges and abundant herbs supported a wealth of prehistoric animals. Reindeer were very prominent in the Upper Pleistocene fauna in cold areas and from 120,000 to 18,000 years ago remains of reindeer are commonly associated with woolly mammoth, hairy rhinoceros, musk ox, cave bear, cave hyena and arctic fox.

As the glaciers retreated during warmer phases, the steppe-tundra and its associated fauna and flora followed them and forests spread up from the south. Whenever warmer, boreal forest phases prevailed, the reindeer withdrew northwards and were replaced by the red deer, a species better adapted for a temperate climate.

In North America caribou increased rapidly during the final cold phase and their range extended as far as Central

America. However, with the warming of the climate they too gradually withdrew northwards as the last continental ice sheet retreated. Caribou in Alaska and reindeer in Eurasia are thought to be among the most successful large mammals of the Pleistocene fauna. Other animals like the woolly mammoth, hairy rhino, cave bear and cave hyena died out at the end of the last Ice Age, but the reindeer and caribou survived the final retreat of the glaciers to their present distribution in the Arctic. Like the extinction of the dinosaurs millions of years before, the disappearance of so many large mammals at the end of the Ice Age has occupied the minds of many scientists. By 10,000 years ago North America had lost more than 70 per cent of its mega-fauna, including the Mastodon and sabre-tooth cats. In Europe a similar loss was experienced, but not on such a large scale; 30,000 years ago large mammals like mammoth, woolly rhino and the giant deer Megaloceros were abundant here, but by 10,500 years ago they were entirely extinct.

These immense extinctions took place over a long period of time and there are a number of theories as to how they came about. An inability to adapt to changing climates and over-hunting by prehistoric man are both thought to have contributed, and it was the larger, slower-breeding species that succumbed. Certainly at the end of the Ice Age the original extensive range for large animals was vastly restricted. In previous warm periods this had not led to extinctions, but combined with the spread of humans equipped with relatively advanced weapons and hunting skills it probably led to the demise of animals unable to adapt quickly enough to changing circumstances.

The cold fauna of today is represented by animals that are confined either to the arctic regions, like reindeer, musk ox, lemming and arctic fox, or to the steppe grasslands of eastern Europe and central Asia, like the saiga antelope and ground squirrel.

These faster-breeding animals are more adaptable to change. They reach sexual maturity at a young age and have a relatively short gestation period, so they are able to react faster to changing environmental conditions. They are also more adaptable in terms of the type of environment they are able to exist in, from boreal forest to tundra, and have the ability to move quickly into new habitats.

L'age du Renne

In Europe the history of reindeer is of particular interest because most ancient reindeer remains are associated with primitive human cultures. Humans of a modern type arrived in western Europe about 35,000 years ago. Upper Palaeolithic man displaced the more primitive Neanderthal and brought with him more sophisticated tools made from wood, stone and bone. Man's existence was intimately bound up with the animals and plants around him as he hunted, fished and collected shellfish, grubs, wild fruits and vegetables.

Upper Palaeolithic people seem to have depended heavily upon reindeer as a source of food and clothing. Kill sites containing many reindeer bones suggest that the animals were extremely important to prehistoric humans. Indeed, at a number of kill sites between 75 and 100 per cent of the total bones present were reindeer. Reindeer also feature heavily in early cave art and rock drawings. About 13,000 years ago, reindeer featured in Palaeolithic art as far south as Altamira in Spain. The seasonal movements of reindeer were also evident at this time, with the human cave-dwellers of the Pyrenees following the migrating herds to the Atlantic and Mediterranean coasts.

All this activity was taking place at a time when glaciation had reached its maximum in Europe, and so the distribution of reindeer was at its most extensive. This led French prehistorians to recognise this era as 'L'age du Renne', suggesting that this was a period of time when reindeer were of the utmost importance to man. In many respects reindeer were the ideal prey. Their seasonal movements were predictable and they used the same crossing places, calving grounds and paths every year, and their curiosity made them easy prey. Their meat provided food, their antlers could be used as tools and their skins could be processed into waterproof and warm clothing.

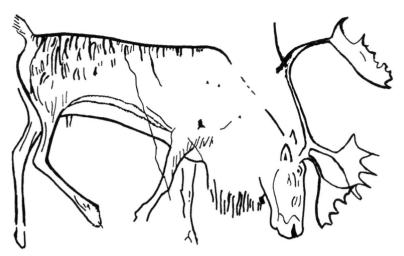

This drawing of a fine reindeer bull was found engraved on a piece of antler dating from the Magdalenian period.

The First Domesticated Animals

The domestication of animals by man is a process generally associated with Neolithic times (5,000 to 2,500 years ago in Europe), when man gradually moved from hunter-gathering to farming. During this transition from a nomadic lifestyle to a sedentary one, a number of our domesticated animals of today were at the beginning of the process of being enclosed by man and so removed from their natural environment. Crop-robbers like cattle and pigs were confined to the human environment and bred in captivity. Cats, which entered human encampments in pursuit of vermin, were selectively bred to produce the domestic cat of today, and in a secondary form of nomadism, after the early sedentary farmers had destroyed their immediate environment, horses and camels were domesticated so man could revert back to a nomadic existence, whereby they once moved with the seasons to find food.

Even before the transition to settled life, there is definite evidence to suggest that some domestication of animals was taking place while man was still basically hunter-gathering. Wolves and man occupied a similar niche and had long pursued similar prey, and it is likely that at least 15,000 years ago the complex social systems of man and wolf teamed up in some loose association to improve hunting techniques to the benefit of both. From the wolf the dog evolved as a hunting companion to man about 6,000 years ago.

The Domestication of Reindeer

As with the wolf/dog, it is quite possible that long before the advent of agriculture there were loose associations between Upper Palaeolithic man and migrating herds of reindeer, associations that could perhaps be regarded as the roots of reindeer domestication. Reindeer were very common at this time, and were easily located and strongly social. Their curious nature meant they were easy to trap, and the early stages of such 'domestication' could well have taken place as long ago as the Upper Palaeolithic period. Reindeer are certainly predisposed to domestication, being highly gregarious animals that tolerate the presence of predators like wolf and man shadowing the herd on the move. Their safety-in-numbers strategy allowed stragglers to be picked off by the predators.

Various theories have been put forward to explain how the domestication of reindeer came about. Initially there must have been some form of social contact between man and beast, perhaps as a result of man hunting his prey, as is thought to be the case with sheep and goats. In the case of sheep and goats the association then became modified following man's quest to settle and farm the land. Like cattle, the sheep and goats were penned up and held back from their seasonal wanderings, instead being fed on the crops that man produced.

The social contact between man and reindeer could well have been accentuated during the winter months when, as described earlier, reindeer are in a state of deprived nutrition, feeding mainly on lichens and eating snow for water. They are known to suffer cravings for minerals and salts during these times and these cravings could well have been put to good use by man. It is well known that reindeer are attracted to human urine, and indeed this is thought to have attracted and bound them to human camps. Supplying salt for them would certainly have emphasised this bond and increased the social contact between man and beast. The use of salt and urine to catch reindeer is well known among reindeer people.

Most forms of animal domestication resulted in the animal being removed from its natural habitat and enclosed, but in the case of reindeer, man and reindeer alike have remained in a nomadic state. This is essential to the well-being of the reindeer because of their highly specialised arctic adaptations. In order to utilise the reindeer as a domesticated animal, man had to accept the animal's natural requirements and allow its nomadic lifestyle to continue.

The Hunter and the Hunted

The reindeer that were attracted to the human camps, even if few in number, could well have helped man to hunt wild reindeer more effectively. It is likely that the early stages of domestication came about as a result of decoy hunting. Various examples of decoy hunting of reindeer have been recorded over the last few hundred years. The ancient Samoyed reindeer herders, for example, hunted wild reindeer by selecting four or five young females from their herd; attaching them to ropes, they would approach a herd of wild reindeer under their cover until the hunter was close enough to shoot his arrow. Another ancient reindeer herding people, the Tungus, adopted a different method. They would leave a few of their tame females on the feeding grounds of wild reindeer during the rutting season, and when the wild males were busy trying to mate with them the Tungus would creep back and shoot them. Another method was to release tame mature bulls during the rut with rope tied round their antlers. During the inevitable tussles with the wild bulls their antlers would become hopelessly entangled and the captured wild reindeer could then be shot.

Driving herds of reindeer into elaborate pitfalls, traps and stockades was an extremely productive hunting method.

Pitfalls were dug on migratory routes at places where the trails were restricted, like narrow valleys, and there is evidence to suggest that movement was further restricted by extensive fences guiding the animals into lines of pitfall traps. Thousands of examples are known, the most extensive ones having as many as 500 pitfalls over a distance of 5 miles. Stockades were another very effective form of hunting on a large scale. Fences radiated out across open ground and were used to drive large herds of deer into a

Migrating reindeer. To live by reindeer man had to become a nomad and follow the moving herds through the seasons.

circular enclosure; once inside the corral they could be either killed or incorporated into already tamed herds.

The tame reindeer were of paramount importance to these processes, and would have been a valuable asset to the hunter. In return he would protect his herd from danger and perhaps actively encourage the tame females to breed with wild males to produce young that would grow up tame. Unintentionally, the hunter would have become a reindeer breeder, but without making any profound changes to the physiology and appearance of the animal. The advantage to a tamed reindeer lay in the protection offered to them by man from predators.

The process of domestication of animals often led to the persecution and eventual extermination of the wild ancestor. However, in the case of reindeer the process of domestication proceeded hand in hand with the continuing hunting of wild reindeer. Indeed, the tame reindeer was a vital team member in the act of hunting his wild cousins.

Why the Caribou Remained Wild

Unlike the reindeer of Eurasia, the caribou of North America were never domesticated. They would undoubtedly have been of prime importance as a hunted animal in Palaeolithic times in North America, but the hunter-gatherer lifestyle appears never to have evolved further, and to this day the indigenous people of North America are hunters rather than herders.

Until the 1950s, when they moved to permanent settlements, the Chipewyan ('caribou-eaters') Indians maximised their contact with caribou by moving from winter settlements in the boreal forest to summer camps near the tree line – a lifestyle reminiscent of the herd-following practices of the early domesticators of reindeer in Eurasia. It appears to have been a successful strategy for survival as the Chipewyan have few legends of starvation, in contrast to the sedentary Inuit on the arctic coastline, who suffered terribly in times of low caribou numbers.

Caribou and wild reindeer today can almost be regarded as a different breed from the domesticated form. As with all truly wild animals, any attempt to tame individual caribou or wild reindeer produces the same problems of stress and agitation that would be found in any wild animal not used to human presence. This has led to a school of thought among Russian scientists that the ancestors of domesticated reindeer today perhaps came from a particular 'race' of reindeer in Eurasia that was predisposed to the process of domestication. Indeed the whole process of domestication is thought by some to be an active process on the part of the animal. By associating themselves with man they passed on the responsibility for escaping their main predator, wolves, thus forming a partnership to the benefit of both sides.

However, the fact that the wild and domesticated forms are so different in their behaviour today could equally be explained by the fact that the process of domestication spans many thousands of years and is not completed in just a few generations. Perhaps the cultures of the North American Indians merely precluded any concept of nurturing the prey, protecting them from predators, or capturing them in corrals to tame or harvest the meat.

Farm Animal of the North

There is considerable debate as to when the hunted wild reindeer became the tame herd animal and indeed when more sophisticated forms of domestication, such as riding, packing, sledge-pulling and milking, evolved. The vast majority of the evidence supporting the transition comes from our cultural history. Drawings in caves and on rocks, finds from archaeological sites and anthropological studies of present-day reindeer-herding people all contribute towards establishing where and when more advanced forms of domestication of reindeer took place. The bones of domesticated reindeer are impossible to tell apart from their wild cousins and so ancient bones are no help in establishing whether the remains are from wild or domesticated reindeer.

The Roots of Reindeer Domestication

Paintings, thought to be 3,000 years old, on the walls of caves beside the River Lena in Russia show humans walking among reindeer but without weapons, suggesting that man was by this time beginning to manipulate and 'herd' the animals. Also thousands of rock paintings and engravings discovered in the Alta Fjord, north Norway, depict various scenes of human activity dating from 4,200 to 500 BC. As well as hunting and fishing scenes, large groups of reindeer are depicted with fences corralling them.

More concrete evidence of reindeer domestication comes from later written accounts in Chinese chronicles. Yao Silian, in his *Chronicles of the Liang Dynasty*, written between 629 and 636, wrote about people living in the northern forests who kept deer instead of cattle and used them to pull 'carriages'. In the *New Book of the Tang Dynasty*, written between 1044 and 1060, mention is made in more detail of a tribe called Ju who lived north of Lake Baikal, 'not having sheep nor horses, but deer', and using the deer to pull carriages. (There was no word for sledge in the Chinese language at that time, and 'carriage' would have been the closest description.)

Certainly it is likely that more sophisticated stages of domestication came about when the reindeer herder came into contact with other herding people or with settled farming folk. It is unclear exactly where and when reindeer were first packed and ridden, although both the Tungus living east of Lake Baikal and the Sayan on the border between Siberia and Mongolia have been described as pioneers in the art of reindeer packing and riding. Whether the two regions developed the practice independently is open to dispute and various contradictory theories have been put forward, based on studies of techniques, styles and equipment. In the mountains of Sayan drawings have been found that indicate man was riding reindeer possibly 2,000 years ago.

From the same region comes indirect evidence for the riding of reindeer in the first millennium BC. The frozen remains of horses were found in the Altai mountains of south Siberia, and one of the horses was equipped with an elaborate mask that appeared to transform the animal into a reindeer with antlers. This 'funeral horse', complete with saddle stuffed with reindeer hair, is thought to be a very superior sort of riding reindeer. The practice of riding reindeer was probably derived from horse culture, since the saddles used for riding reindeer in south Siberia are very similar to horse saddles. Pack saddles for these reindeer were almost definitely derived from the same origins.

However, the ancient Tungus have also been credited by some as the original domesticators of reindeer. The Tungus were the ancestors of many different groups of reindeer hunters and herders in Russia today, including the Evenk, Even and Dolgans. Their extensive spread from their original

An art perfected by the reindeer people of the taiga, here an Evenki woman
rides a reindeer.

territories east of Lake Baikal is an indication of how
successful they were. Like the Sayan, it is very likely that they
developed a method of riding reindeer to enable them to travel
with ease through the taiga, to allow them to hunt and fish.
However, their style of riding was fundamentally different
from that of the people of the Sayan, and instead of riding on
the backs of their reindeer they 'perched' on their shoulders.
For the reindeer this was a much better technique as they have
a relatively weak back compared with horses. In addition, the
Tungus mounted their reindeer from the right instead of the
left side, and used a long pole for balance instead of stirrups.
The Tungus' method of riding was definitely superior and
allowed them to spread far into the Siberian taiga.

No snow needed – elderly Nenet women travelling by reindeer and sledge in early summer.

Packing reindeer for carrying loads almost definitely preceded the technique of riding them and for the Tungus and the Sayan the riding saddle was most probably an adaptation of the pack saddle. However, packing reindeer was also widespread among the reindeer-herding people of northern Europe. The Sami, for example, never rode their reindeer and their type of pack saddle was completely different from those used in south Siberia. It is therefore generally agreed that the two types of reindeer packs evolved independently.

The use of reindeer for pulling sledges is almost universal among the reindeer tribes of the tundra and was almost certainly learnt from dog sledging. The harness used by reindeer herders in east Siberia has strong similarities with a dog harness. Riding reindeer would have been the most practical mode of transport in the boreal forest, but sledging would have been more compatible with the wide-open spaces of the tundra. Indeed, as draft animals reindeer were far superior to dogs not only because they could pull heavier loads but also because they could literally 'feed off the land', grazing from the natural vegetation along the way. As beasts of burden, the reindeer opened up vast areas of otherwise inhospitable land to man. The tundra and taiga could now be utilised by nomadic people travelling easily over long distances to hunt and fish.

Direct suckling of milk from lactating females by herdsmen and children was probably an ancient custom among early herding people but hand-milking to store and cheese-making were probably learnt much later. The reindeer people of north Scandinavia probably copied the practice from Scandinavian farmers because their words for milk, cheese and milking implements are of Germanic origin. Milking was also developed, probably independently, in northern Asia, where again it was probably copied from cattle farmers.

By associating themselves with an animal as superbly adapted to its environment as the reindeer, man was able to move into some of the most inhospitable areas of the world.

From Hunter to Pastoralist

Domesticated reindeer were a vital part of the hunter-gatherer lifestyle that reindeer people pursued. They used the animals not only to access their hunting and fishing grounds but also to carry their belongings as they made their seasonal moves. Only a few reindeer were needed for these tasks but they were so important for this role that they were not regarded as a source of food. Only wild reindeer were killed for their meat and skins. But this modest lifestyle was gradually to change as there was a shift towards keeping larger groups of domesticated reindeer. This seems to have happened independently in many different areas of north Scandinavia and Siberia but a lack of archaeological evidence means the exact timings of the rise of reindeer pastoralism before 1600 is unclear. We do know that it took place some time before 892, because in that year the

Norwegian chieftain Ottar sent a letter to King Alfred of Norway informing him that he owned 600 domestic reindeer.

Certainly by 1600 a system dominated by hunting and fishing but supplemented by small-scale reindeer breeding was prevalent among most native people of the Eurasian tundra. Domesticated reindeer were still exclusively used for transportation, with hunted wild reindeer providing meat and skins for food, household needs, tents and clothing.

It was not until the early eighteenth century that numbers of domestic reindeer began to grow, particularly among the tundra herds, and in the mid- to late 1700s there was a population explosion, with herds increasing tenfold in some cases. Wealthy herders owning over 1,000 reindeer were compared with less wealthy ones having 100 to 200 and poor families with about 20 to 30. As the domestic herds of reindeer grew, so wild reindeer numbers fell and for many of these people the hunting of wild reindeer virtually disappeared.

There are various theories as to why the domestic herds suddenly blossomed over a period of about 150 years. Any increase in numbers would have depended on ecological as well as social factors. Even though the reindeer had been domesticated, they were still totally reliant on the climatic conditions and the quality of natural pastures. Hot dry summers in the tundra are particularly difficult for reindeer, since the resulting poor vegetation means they face the harsh winter in poor condition. And although reindeer are well adapted for temperatures as low as −25 to −30 °C, winters severer than this and with drastic temperature fluctuations take their toll on condition and raise natural mortality. Since wild and domesticated reindeer are physiologically very similar, it is evident that the two populations would thrive or fail under the same natural conditions, and so in this instance the two populations would have increased simultaneously. The knock-on effect of this would be greater numbers of wild reindeer available for hunting, which would alleviate the need to slaughter any domesticated animals. Indeed, many herders, despite owning many reindeer in some cases, strenuously avoided slaughtering their own animals even when they were faced with starvation conditions from lack of animals to hunt or fish. Some herders regarded the hunted or fished animal as their food and their owned reindeer as their wealth. Only in an emergency would they kill a domestic reindeer. And when they *were* forced to slaughter a domesticated reindeer, it had to be done in such a manner as not to spill any blood, otherwise it was considered sinful! The meat from game animals and particularly wild reindeer was considered to be more prestigious than that of the domesticated reindeer, to which many herders were indifferent. The tradition of conserving as many domestic reindeer as possible was deeply embedded and probably helped to accumulate huge herds of domesticated animals, which would eventually evolve into a food-producing reindeer economy.

The transition to a meat-producing economy took place simultaneously among many different tundra nomads, from the Sami in the west to the Koriak and Chukchi in the far east, where both groups amassed large herds. Although this accumulation of domesticated reindeer was partly a response to demands for meat, it could also have been because of a need for reindeer skins. Meat could be obtained from hunting game but there was virtually no substitute for reindeer skins. And not just any old skin! Skins from reindeer slaughtered at different times of year and at different ages were all required to meet the demands of the herders' everyday life. A special slaughter in July produced the short-haired skins needed for the inside set of winter clothing, while early winter kills provided the thicker coats needed to make inner sleeping chambers for tents. Skins from the latest slaughter in October were necessary for the very warmest clothes, needed when winter hunting for sea mammals, a practice which involved long hours sitting out on the ice. The lack of any of these particular types of skin would have jeopardised the very existence of these peoples.

Whatever the reason for the increasing size of domestic herds, harvesting meat from a herd of domesticated reindeer was a much more reliable source of food than hunting wild reindeer and led to increasing numbers of indigenous people. In turn, this led to increased competition for grazing with the wild reindeer. They still led a nomadic life, but now the herders followed a specific herd of reindeer as opposed to hunting only the wild ones.

Any surplus of reindeer meat and skins meant the herders could trade and barter with other people. In the early 1800s the Komi reindeer breeders were known to kill regularly large numbers of reindeer and use the meat and skins to 'buy' goods such as flour or butter and to pay hired labour. The Chukchi and Koryak also began to trade with the coastal communities, supplying them with reindeer meat and skins. The coastal hunters suffered from the declining numbers of wild reindeer, which all but vanished from the far east of Russia as the domestic herds grew. The size of the domestic herds varied, people of the tundra tending to keep larger numbers of animals than the people of the boreal forest. No doubt this reflected the more solitary habits of the forest reindeer compared with the more gregarious tundra reindeer. Regardless of the ways in which these different people used their reindeer, with them man could live and thrive in the arctic and sub-arctic areas of the world. The reindeer became their cows, sheep and horses – three animals for the price of one!

The Product of Domestication

As a result of domestication and selective breeding the domesticated animal is quite often very different in appearance to its wild relative. The average pink pig is a far cry from its ancestor the wild boar. A lack of hair, a shortened snout, a long (bacon-producing) back and a curly tail are all physical traits that have come about as a result of selecting for tameness, increased fecundity and a fast-growing meat-producing carcass.

Change of coat colour from the wild type and variety of colour within a species is one of the most conspicuous effects of domestication. Cattle, horses, dogs, goats and sheep, for example, are all found today in various combinations of black, white and brown, spotted, striped and speckled. Change in coat structure also occurs, with hairlessness, lengthening of hair and increased woolliness of coat all being known. Size too is often affected, with the early forms of domesticated animals certainly appearing smaller than their wild ancestors, although examples of oversize can also be a product of domestication.

Changes to the skull and skeleton are also seen, with a shortening of the nose, lengthening of the tail and either a lengthening or shortening of the limbs, all resulting from intense selection which has far removed the product from its roots. Many characteristics of domestication are in reality juvenile traits that have persisted to adulthood. The shortening of the skull in particular is a hangover from the juvenile form.

Russian scientists looking at the process of domestication experimented with silver foxes. Though kept in captivity to harvest its fur, the silver fox is basically a wild animal. In a population of caged silver foxes they selected for one trait, tameness. Any fox that showed any signs of friendliness was kept and allowed to breed, while any that exhibited wild behaviour like snarling from the back of the cage was killed. Within just a few generations the scientists had effectively bred a 'dog-like fox' that was multi-coloured, had a shortened snout, had folded instead of pointed ears and barked like a dog.

The Domesticated Reindeer

Domesticated herds of reindeer show a substantial amount of colour variation compared with wild herds. The majority will be the normal grey/brown colour, but there will also be a few examples at each end of the colour spectrum, ranging from white to black reindeer, with various gradations in between. Domesticated reindeer are also found to be piebald (with dark and light patches) and a 'salt and pepper' type, which has light-coloured guard hairs over a basically dark coat. The colour variation is particularly obvious in newly born calves, which can vary from jet black to pure white.

Domesticated reindeer generally have a shorter muzzle than their wild cousins and are invariably smaller in body and stature. However, in contrast to the vast majority of farm animals domesticated reindeer still look remarkably similar to the wild ones. They readily interbreed, and have the same

Unlike their wild cousins, domesticated reindeer show considerable colour variation from pure white through to jet black.

holarctic distribution as their wild cousins. Selective breeding has not been as intense a process in reindeer because they are so perfectly adapted to the environment they evolved to thrive in. If allowed to go wild, domesticated reindeer would quickly revert to the original wild state of thousands of generations ago.

Reindeer Cultures

The indigenous people of the Arctic and sub-Arctic represent the most extensive spread of native people in the world today. In north Russia alone they span an area of some 6,000km, from the Finnish/Russian border in the west to the Pacific Ocean and Bering Straits in the east. At the western end the north–south belt is 1,000km wide, broadening to 3,000km at the Pacific. Although ethnically and culturally different, the majority of the indigenous people of north Russia, north Scandinavia, the North American Arctic and Greenland share a common dependency on reindeer or caribou, whether domesticated or wild.

In north Russia a total population of approximately 180,000 belong to about 30 different indigenous groups who live in small permanent or temporary settlements close to their subsistence grounds of reindeer herding, wild animal hunting and fishing. Approximately 30,000 Sami of north Norway, Sweden, Finland and the Kola peninsula in Russia also practise reindeer herding with hunting and fishing supplementing their incomes. Finally the native people east of the Bering Straits total about 125,000 in number. Today known collectively as the Inuit, these people live in coastal areas from Alaska across arctic Canada to Greenland, hunting marine mammals, fishing and 'harvesting' migrating herds of caribou.

For the anthropologist the various reindeer people, whether nomads, pastoralists, pastoral nomads or hunter-gatherers, offer a fantastic opportunity which has led to many expeditions over the last few hundred years to study their traditional ways of life in the Arctic and sub-Arctic. Throughout this region of the world there are different reindeer people derived from various ancestral cultures, the origins of which have been extensively researched through the study of their dress, language, the way they utilise their reindeer, and the extent to which hunting and fishing contribute to their daily existence.

As well as developing their own distinct cultures there has inevitably been considerable intermingling and assimilation between groups, and different groups often evolved a combination of various practices to suit their immediate environment. For the archaeologist the lifestyle of many of these people continues to reflect a moment in history when the hunter-gatherer was evolving into a farmer. Studying their hunting techniques, gathering methods and unique subsistence lifestyle helps to illustrate how man evolved. Anthropological studies over the past few centuries have provided a wealth of information to show how such people lived.

Reindeer People of the Siberian Taiga

Siberia is at the same latitudes as northern Europe and Canada but the huge landmass of Eurasia means the range of temperatures there is much more extreme than in Canada, with average winter temperatures between −30 and −40 °C. In fact the coldest place in the world is Verkhoyansk in north-east Siberia, where the temperature can drop as low as −71 °C. In stark contrast, the summer temperatures can rise to as high as +34 °C.

The Evenki (also spelt Evenk) and Even are both descendants of the ancient Tungus people who traditionally used their reindeer solely as beasts of burden, only slaughtering them in exceptional circumstances. The original range of the Tungus embraced the whole of south-eastern Siberia as well as northern Manchuria and Mongolia, a vast area covering more than 2 million square miles. Regarded by many as the original domesticators of reindeer, the Tungus were a highly successful race who penetrated vast areas of the Siberian taiga with their nomadic hunting way of life. The

On the move. The Dolgan, a relatively new race of reindeer people and renowned for their more 'modern' outlook on reindeer-herding life, have perfected the *balok*, a light mobile, furnished home. Pulled by a team of reindeer, it makes for comfortable travel across the tundra.

average herd size for a family would be perhaps thirty or forty reindeer, with individual animals being familiar to the herders and kept close to the camp. The reindeer of these taiga people were regarded as the tamest of all domesticated reindeer, and they enjoyed various luxuries such as 'smudge fires', the smoke from which helped to keep mosquitoes away, salt during the winter months and protection from predators. In return, the reindeer provided rich milk, a reliable mode of transport and the perfect hunting accomplice.

To provide the reindeer with the best grazing through the changing season, the herders needed to follow a completely nomadic way of life, with summer pastures up on the watersheds and winter grazing down in the river basin. This pattern reflected the natural requirements of their forest reindeer. They lived in easily transportable conical tents, like North American tepees, covered with reindeer skins or birch bark. This type of dwelling is very common among all nomadic people of the north. The Even, in particular, were renowned for owning large, strong and durable reindeer, which were highly valued and sought after by other reindeer-herding people.

As well as using reindeer as domesticated animals, these people also hunted wild reindeer for food. Communal spirit was strong among these people, and the spoils from a hunt were shared among the whole group in a custom which the Tungus called *nimat*. Indeed, the reindeer were owned communally. There was a general adherence to mutual assistance and storehouses set up at various points through the forest were available to all.

The Evenki are one of the largest groups of indigenous people of the taiga and are widespread in central and eastern Siberia. The Even are to be found in the Russian far east. An adaptable race, these people have encompassed new practices such as raising livestock when the immediate environment was appropriate. In south Siberia reindeer herders encountered other ways of living which has led them to mix elements of different lifestyles to suit their own circumstances. Yak, horse, sheep, goat and cattle have often been incorporated into Evenki cultures. In the north, beyond the taiga and into the tundra, the Tungus either ousted or absorbed the locals and adopted elements of their way of life; from this emerged a 'new' race of reindeer people, the Dolgans. In north-east Russia the Evens also adopted facets of other reindeer cultures, including dog sleds, sea-mammal hunting and semi-permanent dwellings.

Alaska's Nearest Neighbours

The Bering Straits, a sea passage just 70km wide, separates Alaska from Russia's north-east fringe, the Chukchi peninsula. The entire peninsula is situated north of the tree line and its vegetation is typically tundra flora. Surrounded on three sides by sea, the climate is maritime and relatively warm, with high precipitation all year round producing deep snow in the winter. Fluctuating temperatures often cause freeze–thaw conditions in winter and a severe wind-chill factor. The indigenous inhabitants of this land are the Chukchi, who herd reindeer inland and on the coast hunt sea mammals and fish. They remained undiscovered by European Russians until the mid-seventeenth century, but evidence of human habitation here dates back at least 10,000 years, with finds of specialised tools associated with sea-mammal hunting dating back to 5,000–3,000 BC.

Chukotkan reindeer herding was first documented by invading Russians in 1648. Early accounts describe the inland Chukchi as keeping reindeer to pull sledges, eating their meat and using their skins for clothing and tents. The reindeer kept by the Chukchi and their closest neighbours the Koryaks were never milked and never ridden. Leading a nomadic life, they accompanied their herds of reindeer on migration between the inland forest tundra and the coastal tundra. They lived in large tents up to 25ft in diameter, with vertical sides and a conical top; the poles crossed at the apex and there was a hole to let the smoke out. Internally the tent was partitioned with skins to provide warmer areas.

Less domesticated than those of the Tungus, the reindeer of the Chukchi and Koryaks remained semi-wild and had to be caught using human urine. Most reindeer in winter crave urine and the herdsmen would carry a flask of urine on their belts in preparation for catching animals to harness up to sledges. Similarities in harness indicate that the art of sledge-pulling by reindeer was almost definitely learnt from the coastal Chukchi and Siberian Yupik peoples, who like the Inuit of Alaska, Canada and Greenland use dogs to pull sledges. The Chukchi could never be described as soft-hearted when handling their reindeer. The more awkwardly the reindeer behaved, the more harshly the Chukchi treated them. They were known to tie them up for days on end until they were broken and ready to be attached to a sledge.

The Chukchi and Koryaks are renowned for keeping large numbers of reindeer, often numbering thousands, a practice that reached its fullest development in the eighteenth and nineteenth centuries. The herding of the reindeer was done by men on foot, without the use of dogs. However, the traditional dress of the Koryak included a wolf-fur hood with 'ears', which presumably frightened the vast herds into staying together.

Often perceived as very prosperous compared with their coastal-living cousins who did not keep reindeer, these reindeer herders themselves believed they occupied an enviable position among the native people of the Russian tundra. The people who lived this way called themselves 'rich in reindeer'. With a constant supply of meat available from their domestic reindeer, tundra-living reindeer herders seldom experienced starvation conditions like the sedentary communities on the arctic coast, who relied heavily on hunting sea mammals and fish. Indeed, on occasions the reindeer herders saved the lives of such people by providing reindeer meat in times of famine.

Wealth among these reindeer herders was traditionally measured in the number of owned reindeer and was reflected in the amount of domestic reindeer eaten by different families. Rich families ate almost exclusively reindeer from their own herds, while poorer families had to supplement their diet by hunting, fishing and gathering their food. This disparity was particularly pronounced among the Chuckchi and Koryak, where wealthy owners ate up to three times as much reindeer meat as the poorer families. Of course, the more reindeer a family owned, the more focused they were on reindeer herding and the more time they spent with their animals; conversely, poorer families spent more time fishing, hunting and gathering their food. Rather than hunt, richer families would trade reindeer meat for food items hunted or gathered by the poorer people. Rich herders would often employ poorer Chukchi to herd their reindeer, paying them in reindeer meat. The Chukchi had a saying: 'If you are young and poor, you must run much and sleep little.'

Despite keeping very large numbers of reindeer, the Chukchi had a very poorly developed counting system. Indeed, their arithmetic was so undeveloped that a rich Chukchi did not really know how many reindeer he owned. They counted in orders of 5, 'like 1 hand', 'like 2 hands' (10) and 'like the man' (20). For 15 they clasped their hands round a single knee and for 20 put their hands round both knees. For 100 reindeer, the description was '5 people, all fingers and toes included'!

Samoyed People and Dogs

The original people of the Russian coastal and forest tundra west of the River Lena, including the Taimyr and Yamal peninsulas, were Samoyeds, a term that some historians interpreted to mean 'self-eater', perhaps because they mistook their fondness for raw reindeer meat and blood as cannibalism.The reindeer-herding Samoyeds traditionally used dogs to herd their reindeer and guard them against predators like wolves and bears. Treated like members of the family, the dogs held a very privileged position among the reindeer herders, even being known to share their food and sleeping quarters. At times when it was impossible to use the reindeer these dogs pulled sledges and even towed fishing boats. The Norwegian explorer Fridtjof Nansen, recognising their usefulness, was one of the first to use Samoyed dogs as draught animals on an expedition. Samoyed dogs went on to accompany a number of expeditions to the Arctic and Antarctic. The breed was introduced into Britain in 1908 and went on to become well known all over the world.

Among the Samoyed peoples of the tundra three groups can be distinguished by language and culture. They are the Nganasan, reindeer hunters of the Taimyr peninsula; their western neighbours the Enets, also traditionally wild reindeer hunters; and further west again the Nenets, one of the most successful indigenous groups of north Russia today. They are found on both sides of the Ural mountain range and on the Yamal peninsula.

For the Nenets reindeer breeding is their main occupation and the most fundamental element of their culture. Tundra Nenets are renowned for the vast distances they travel with their herds, sometimes trekking hundreds of miles between the coastal tundra in summer, to benefit from the profusion of vegetation for their reindeer, and the forest tundra in winter, where there is abundant lichen for the reindeer and plentiful wood for fuel. Among the Nenets the accumulation of large herds of domesticated reindeer, as with the Chukchi and Koryak, began to take place during the seventeenth century. Individual status was again determined by the number of reindeer in a man's possession, an owner of more

Among the Nenet, dogs are treated like one of the family.

than 1,000 reindeer being considered rich. Within a migrating herd the distance that individual families travelled with their reindeer also varied, with the richer families usually migrating considerably further than the poorer ones, but richness was precarious and disease or bad weather could sometimes result in sudden losses. In a similar system to the Chukchi's mutual assistance, poorer herders 'earned' their reindeer meat by hunting and fishing.

Sami People of North Scandinavia and Russia

Probably the most well-known type of reindeer herding is the Sami or Lappish method in Lapland, an area stretching across the north of Norway, Sweden, Finland and European Russia. The name Lapp derives from a Finnish word which can be translated as 'outcast', and so these people, once generally referred to as Lapps, now prefer to be called Sami. Like other reindeer herders in Eurasia, they began as hunters of reindeer, and particularly effective hunters they were. Indeed, their skill eventually led to the demise of wild reindeer in Lapland and the Sami were then forced to live with their domesticated herds alone. The most striking feature of their hunting techniques was the sheer size of the herds involved, as described in eyewitness accounts and evidenced by the remains of vast trapping systems all over north Scandinavia. Remains of pitfall traps and stockades are found all over Lapland. Located on migration routes at restricted points such as narrow valleys, all the pits were oval and steep-sided, and were inlaid with flattened stones to prevent the trapped animal from climbing out. Many pitfall sites have been researched, with some turning out to be very extensive. For example, at one site in a valley between the Varanga Fjord and the Tana River fifteen separate groups of pitfalls have been discovered. In all, there were 2,426 traps. Stockades were also extremely effective and descriptions of them have been found from the mid-seventeenth century. Some of these old hunting stockades have been modified and are still in use today to gather domesticated herds. At its heart was a circular enclosure, often based on a natural feature, such as a slope below a crag, from which spur fences radiated away to direct the herds of reindeer into the enclosure or stockade, where they would be killed or captured. Although many accounts of numbers were probably exaggerated, the large quantity of evidence suggests a huge abundance of reindeer.

The Sami practised different degrees of pastoral nomadism, depending on their immediate circumstances. Those living in the mountains undertook long seasonal migrations between summer and winter grazing, accumulated relatively large herds, which they relied on for meat and skins, and used draught reindeer which they packed or used to pull sledges. At the other end of the spectrum the forest Sami kept fewer animals and had greater control over their reindeer; they embarked on only short migrations, reflecting the nature of the forest reindeer. Neat distinctions, however, should be avoided as there was inevitably a large amount of overlap between the two types of herding.

The Sami traditionally drove their herds using a decoy reindeer, a trained castrated male led by a man. The main herd would then follow him, urged on by men and dogs

Some things never change – the Sami method of herding traditionally uses a decoy reindeer to lead the herd.

herding them from behind. This decoy reindeer was no doubt a remnant from their hunting past. Equipped with skis (which they are credited with inventing), the Sami could even move their herds during periods of snow cover. Sledges laden with their household needs were drawn by reindeer during the months of snow, while for the rest of the year they used packs. The Sami never developed a technique of riding their reindeer, although they did transport their babies in cradles on the backs of reindeer.

Shamanism

Man has been associated with reindeer for many thousands of years. They were a 'meal ticket' for pioneers moving into inhospitable areas like the Arctic. They were indispensable to man, not only as a source of food and a beast of burden, but ultimately as an animal that would help transport the shaman or witch doctor into the spiritual world to seek advice on daily matters such as disease, fertility and weather. Indeed, shaman is a Tungus word, and shamanism remains an extremely important aspect of life among reindeer herding and hunting people. These people practised various forms of shamanist religion, believing that all natural things, whether they be animals, rocks, mountains or plants, had spirits. The shaman performed religious rites to connect with the spirit world, projecting his soul and flying there. In a trance-induced dance, created by beating a special drum, the shaman, dressed in a fine costume adorned with various representations of his or her 'helper', which might be a deer, a bear or a bird, would pass out of the middle world to communicate with the spirits. In particular the shaman was believed to be able to cure his people of disease. His soul-flights to the spirits were also performed to influence hunting success and fertility. In Nenet cultures they believe the drum is a 'sacred reindeer' that transports the shaman to the other worlds. Their view is that the world is densely populated by various spirits, both evil and benevolent. Evil spirits make people sick, or kill them, disperse the reindeer and sometimes decimate the herds. Benevolent or guardian spirits live nearby and protect the family and reindeer.

The killing of animals and trees was only permitted by nature if it was necessary for human survival. These people therefore held a certain reverence towards the animals they hunted. Magic drums, wooden and stone effigies and sacred and sacrificial sites were all typical features of their religion, in which reindeer played a pivotal role.

Hobson's Choice

The Evenki, Chukchi, Koryak, Nenet and Sami illustrate some of the different ways in which man has utilised reindeer in order to be able to live in these northern areas. Many more tribes, which are culturally and linguistically distinct, could be cited. What emerges from any study of these people is the similarities between many of their methods; this has led people to suggest that the art of reindeer herding evolved in the south of Siberia and then spread eventually to every corner of the range, reaching west to Scandinavia and east to the Chukchi peninsula. Certainly there is common ground among many of these different people. For example, the vast majority used a 'tepee-like' conical tent as a transportable home. For many, the ownership of reindeer was determined by ear marking and lassos originally made of reindeer sinews or sealskin were widely used among the tundra reindeer herders for catching reindeer. A trait common to *all* the reindeer-herding peoples involves an annual migration of varying length to the coastal or mountain tundra in the summer and back again for the winter to where lichen is available for the reindeer to graze. Although some techniques could well have been learnt from neighbouring tribes, the overwhelming evidence today suggests that reindeer herding evolved independently at various locations across Eurasia. The parameters for diversification would have been limited because of the environmental constraints of the arctic and sub-arctic climate and the necessity to keep the reindeer in their natural state for them to thrive. Hence Hobson's choice, there was simply no other way to do it!

Today's Reindeer Herders

As with many of the indigenous peoples around the world, the rights of the reindeer herders have all too often been neglected and invading armies regularly forced these people to move northwards to less hospitable territories. Indeed, many of the original reindeer-herding people have had their lives irreversibly changed through industrialisation, urbanisation and ideological practices. Where herding reindeer was once a traditional way of life for many, now their culture and practices have been diminished by various outside pressures, usually beyond their control. Some have coped relatively well with changing attitudes and the encroachment of the modern world and technology, but many indigenous minorities have not fared so well and in a few cases their whole social system has been completely destroyed.

The reindeer herders and hunters of Siberia were initially exploited by the Tsarist empire to pay *yasak*, a tax in animal furs, and this was followed by the sweeping changes brought in by the ideological beliefs of Soviet Russia. The aim of the

Soviet era was to eliminate ethnic differences and apply strict classlessness, which inevitably turned the clan structure of these indigenous peoples upside down. Natural leaders, wealthy reindeer owners and shaman were regarded as exploiters and thus were persecuted and excluded from political society. *Nimat*, the sharing of hunted food, could be regarded as a primitive form of communism but the newly formed communist regime did not see it like this and considered it a disguised form of exploitation and social parasitism. Collectivisation, relocation, spiritual oppression and destruction of social patterns and values were all products of Soviet communism. The vast majority of the reindeer herders were obliged to give up their nomadic life and move into collective farms or towns. The only language tolerated was Russian and the children of the reindeer people were sent away to boarding schools, thus breaking the links between them and their elders. Inevitably the people became completely dependent on the communist system, which supplied them with all their everyday needs, including food and medical supplies, and a market for the meat from their domestic herds of reindeer and whatever they could hunt. In defence of the communist system, though, the lives of women were hugely improved under the new regime as many taboos were broken, particularly relating to childbirth and exclusion from public decision-making.

With the recent change to a market economy as a result of perestroika, the reindeer people who were forced to become dependent on the state system have now been left with nothing. With the breakdown of the supply and transport systems to these remote areas, these people are in desperate straits; they have no medical supplies, no food supplies, no source of income and no legal expertise to deal with the situation. Those who choose to go back to their traditional way of life are faced all too often with the destruction and degradation of the environment because of the communist regime's disregard for nature in their bid to industrialise the north, extract minerals, oil and gas reserves, fell forests and wantonly exploit nuclear energy. It would seem to be an impossible situation, but they are proud people with great endurance, no doubt partly because of the extreme environment they inhabit. Some groups have already won ground nationally and internationally, and campaigners particularly interested in the environmental issues see the native people and their way of life as vitally important in restoring the natural environment.

The Sami of northern Europe have also been discriminated against, particularly where their way of life proved an obstacle to modernisation, agriculture and industrialisation. Their culture was all too often regarded as primitive and in many cases their language and lifestyle were suppressed or banned. Swedish Sami families were relocated in the 1920s when the national border between Norway and Sweden was closed. The traditional migration routes to the coast were closed, and the Sami were relocated by the Swedish government further inland. However, although they have not been treated well in the past, the Sami today have more political clout than ever before and are coping relatively well with the changes imposed on their culture.

The World's Tamest Reindeer

Some years ago a reindeer expert from Tromso University in Norway came to see our reindeer here in Scotland, and on leaving he commented, 'I think you probably have the tamest reindeer in the world.' After a visit to the Tsataan, Mongolia's only reindeer people, I'm not so sure he is right.

Most people imagine Outer Mongolia as either a desert full of dinosaur bones and camels or vast grasslands full of cows, sheep, goats, yaks and horses. They would all be right, because 95 per cent of Mongolia is precisely that, but the last 5 per cent in the north is taiga, part of the great northern boreal forest that stretches the length and breadth of Siberia. The border with Mongolia cuts through the very southern reaches of it.

The First Reindeer Domesticators

Often referred to as the earliest centre of reindeer breeding and herding in the world, the Eastern Sayan Mountains of south Siberia and north Mongolia are home to the most southerly located populations of reindeer-herding peoples, the Tofa, Tozhu, Soyot and Dukha. They are closely related and their ancestors were hunter-gatherers who came from western Siberia about 2000 BC. Reindeer are vital to the everyday life of these people, as a means of transport, as pack and riding animals and as a source of milk. Particularly in the summer when the biting flies torment them, the reindeer stay close to the camp where the herders build 'smudge fires', the smoke of which helps to keep mosquitoes away. The male reindeer are highly valued and very seldom eaten. Indeed, there is a saying among these people, 'you must not eat the reindeer that you ride'. Many of these indigenous peoples have lost their reindeer culture now and those actively involved in reindeer herding today are few in number. There are thought to be only thirty families in Mongolia that still live by their reindeer and a family may own as few as ten reindeer each. Their long-term future is severely threatened. Many of the Tofa, Tozhu and Soyot are no longer actively involved in reindeer herding because their culture was so severely suppressed by Soviet Communism and the damage is beyond repair.

Travelling to the Tsataan

The Dukha or Tsataan (the Mongolian word for reindeer people) are restricted to north-west Mongolia where they fled in the 1930s as Soviet rule took over in Russia. I have always been fascinated by the Tsataan, who still live very traditional lives, largely untouched by modernisation. With Mongolia now free of the grip of Communism, it is a country that is relatively easy to visit. However, getting to these people was an ordeal in itself. Having rustled up a couple of travelling companions – my son Alex, who was keen to see Mongolia, and his girlfriend Jess, who was fanatical about horse riding in any shape or form – we made our plans and soon found ourselves on a flight to Mongolia via Beijing. Outer Mongolia is a vast country and following a 2-hour internal flight from the capital Ulanbataar, we experienced our first Mongolian jeep ride. A 3-hour-long head-banging, bone-shaking journey brought us to the small town of Khatgal, situated at the southern end of Lake Khovsgol, Mongolia's largest lake.

This was to be our first night in a *ger*, the traditional nomad's home. There was a central wood-burning stove in the felt-covered circular tent, and the only window was in the roof, where the chimney went out, and incidentally the rain comes in. After a meal of traditional Mongolian food, mutton and noodle soup, we fell into our beds for a very welcome night's sleep.

The next day the weather was perfect, hot and sunny with a slight cooling breeze. It was warm and dry enough for us to question the need for all our thermal clothing, waterproofs, hats and gloves. Shorts and t-shirts seemed to be the order of the day in 'the land of the blue skies', as Mongolia describes itself to tourists.

The only way to travel into the outer reaches of Mongolia is on horseback, and where the jeep tracks end, the horse trails begin. So a group of Mongolian horses was to be our mode of transport for the next fourteen days on our journey to the Tsataan and back.

It was only on the eighth day, after averaging 8 hours' riding each day, that we reached 'reindeer country'. Quite abruptly the habitat changed, the grasslands ceased and the taiga began. A full day's riding through sinking bog was enough to make us wonder if we were ever going to reach our destination, and perhaps more urgently, where we were going to pitch our tent that night because we didn't particularly want to get wet.

As we headed north up another river valley the terrain underfoot suddenly improved as we followed a very obvious stony path. As we wound our way through the larch trees the valley floor suddenly opened up in front of us, and to our relief and general excitement we saw conical-shaped tents and a few tethered reindeer in the distance. This was the Tsataan's autumn camp. Thirteen families lived here, in what seemed like a tiny island in an ocean of tree scrub. Their chosen autumn grazing for their reindeer was adjacent to a broad, shallow river, and the whole valley floor was full of birch and willow scrub, which extended up the gently rolling hills on each side until it gave way to shorter tundra-type vegetation at the top, at an altitude of about 2,000m. It was up in the mountain tundra that the Tsataan spent the early summer, when the reindeer benefited from the rich mountain pastures. Their autumn camp lay halfway between the summer and winter grazing, with the reindeer busily seeking out the forest mushrooms that grew all around.

As we unpacked the horses and began to put up our tents for the night, two old ladies came over to see who we were. Our conversational Mongolian was non-existent, so we were only able to say a welcoming hello, but our guide Butsuuri

A Tsataan camp, Outer Mongolia, located beside a river for water, a mature forest for firewood and amidst a carpet of willow and birch scrub for reindeer. This cluster of conical tents is home to thirteen families.

was able to explain briefly where we came from and our interest in their reindeer. I hoped they didn't mind complete strangers coming to their camp. However, we had brought warm clothes that we intended to leave behind, along with several bags of flour that we had purchased at the last town, Tsagaan Nuur, flour being their staple diet along with reindeer milk and meat.

We had arrived late in the evening and it was evident that all their reindeer were tethered for the night between the conical tents. There were two obvious groups of reindeer. The biggest group numbered about thirty and the other group about fifteen. All were tethered to larch timbers lying flat on the ground. The ground around the reindeer was quite worn and they would clearly have to wait until morning before they would get anything to eat.

By the time we had unpacked and erected the tents, darkness was nearly upon us, but there was still enough time to wander across and enjoy the sunset with the sleepy reindeer, chewing the cud and dozing off for the night. The tranquil scene was everything I had hoped for. As it was autumn, the reindeer, like the vegetation around them, were changing colour as the lighter-coloured winter coat began to grow through the short dark summer coat. The one breeding bull had a full set of hard antlers, the velvet already stripped from them ready for the rutting season. Beside him rested a beautiful white castrated male, still in full velvet. The rest of the group appeared to be mainly cows and calves, although judging by the size of their antlers I felt sure some of them must be young bulls that had not yet shed the velvet on their antlers. In fact, they were nearly all cows, with very impressive antlers. The younger bulls and cows without calves were still higher up in the mountains at this time of year, tended by other family members. Completely contented in their surroundings, these tethered reindeer didn't move a muscle when we walked in among them. They were almost in a trance, unflinching when we stroked them and virtually oblivious to our existence.

I had chosen the autumn to go and visit them because by that time in the year the reindeer would be looking their best, with full sets of antlers and in good condition ready for the winter. I was certainly not disappointed by the reindeer. As they were forest reindeer I expected them to grow quite flat antlers with many points, and this was the case. Their antlers were the most beautiful I had ever seen. Even the calves had impressive antlers. These reindeer also had a quietness and patience about them, which I see in our own reindeer particularly when I handle them at Christmas time. But these reindeer were even more relaxed than ours in Scotland, reflecting the trust that has developed over thousands of years in this area, and the incredibly intimate bond between reindeer and man.

Daily Routine

The next morning I got up early to make sure I didn't miss anything. It was a bright sunny morning and there appeared to be no sign of life in the camp. But soon two young women emerged from separate tents and moved quietly through the two groups of reindeer, milking each cow in turn. First they hobbled her front legs with a short piece of rope to prevent the cow from moving off, and then they quickly set to drawing any milk out of the four-chambered udder. The cows stood absolutely still, not moving an inch and never attempting to kick over the small urns that the girls were squirting the milk

The first chore of the day at the Tsataan camp – milking the reindeer.

into. Each cow took about 10 minutes to milk, the calf alongside straining at its tether when it smelt its mother's milk. Eleven cows produced enough milk almost to fill two 1-litre urns. It seemed a tiny amount of milk for over an hour's work! This milk was used in traditional Mongolian tea, made very weak with plenty of milk and salt added. Any surplus would be made into a very hard cheese that could be eaten at a later date when fresh milk was no longer available.

With the milking finished, the routine for the rest of the day unfolded in front of our eyes. The adult reindeer, cows, bulls and castrates, were released first, still wearing their simple halters but with the lead rein tied loosely around their necks. Three or four at a time were released and shooed in the direction the owners wanted them to go that day. As soon as each individual was released they ran off quickly, browsing hungrily on the leaves of nearby scrub. Constantly on the move, they nipped off leaves here and there, at the same time making a bee-line away from the camp and into the surrounding forest. Within minutes the adult reindeer had vanished from sight, with only a few stragglers to indicate the direction they had taken.

As the adults were released, the calves grunted persistently, each indicating its displeasure at its mother's sudden departure and indicating its desire to follow her. With the adults away the camp seemed empty. The daily chores of shaking out last night's bedding, gathering firewood and dealing with the day's milk all took place before the calves, still grunting, were let off their tether ropes. With their mothers away the calves ran around like headless chickens, not knowing where to go and not daring to venture far from the camp. They eventually settled down, eating leaves and investigating the immediate camp surrounds. Their inquisitiveness brought them across to our tents and our horses tethered beside them. Like any young animals, there was an element of playfulness about them, as they pawed at the base of our tents and investigated our fireplace. Once their curiosity was satisfied they pottered off to fill their bellies with vegetation. Although the birch leaves were already turning colour, there would still be a lot of goodness in them, and in the willow leaves. Down by the river, however, there were some grasses that the calves seemed to be particularly keen to find, nuzzling around the stones and even dislodging some with their noses to get every last morsel. The Tsataan later told us that they like to bring their reindeer here in the autumn for a particular grass, which on closer study looked to me like marestail or equisetum. They also came here for the abundance of mushrooms, which the adult reindeer would be searching for in the surrounding taiga.

During the middle of the day, while the reindeer were all away gorging themselves in the surrounding forest, the two young women who had earlier milked the reindeer headed on to the nearby slopes to collect cowberries. These bright red berries, sour in taste and with a leathery leaf, were abundant across the forest floor. We offered to help pick them, but it was a particularly laborious job, since each individual berry was only the size of a small redcurrant. While we picked the small berries one by one into a cup, the women used a slightly more effective 'comb', which plucked a few berries each time it was swept across the plants. Regardless of the method, the task was slow and over a couple of hours the five of us only managed to collect about 2kg. The Tsataan collect the berries to sell to Chinese traders, who use them in medicines for respiratory problems. At 1,000 Tugrugs per kg (about 50p), it was hardly rewarding for an afternoon's work for five people.

In late afternoon the adult reindeer appeared from the forest, led by the cows presumably seeking out their calves. Their arrival was spotted not only by the calves, eager to get a suckle of milk, but also by the young women who had released them earlier in the day. The two women headed quickly across the river to where the reindeer were grazing and quickly caught each one, tempting them with small bags of rock salt and tethering them individually to small rocks or shrubbery. The point of attachment did not appear to be particularly secure, but then the reindeer didn't really look as if they were going anywhere, the daily routine being so engrained into their lives. The calves, happy to see their mothers again, needed no tethering to keep them there. The reindeer's liking for salt interested me, because I had rather assumed that this was a craving restricted to the winter months when the reindeer have to rely on nutrient-deficient lichens for food. But that was definitely not the case here, where despite the abundance of food the reindeer were well and truly addicted to salt. In the evening, once all the reindeer were back from the forest, the herd was led back across the river to their overnight tethering spots beside the tents, where the calves were also tethered for the night to prevent them suckling their mother's milk. Each day followed a very similar pattern of events, the only variation being the time at which the adult reindeer returned from the forest. But, like clockwork, they always returned to the safe haven of the camp for the night.

Tsataan dogs wandered freely around the tents, weaving among the tethered reindeer. Neither took any notice of the other. Dogs didn't appear to have any role in terms of herding the reindeer but no doubt their mere presence around the camp day and night helped to protect the reindeer from wolf predation. Wolves would certainly be a problem for the Tsataan, the taiga being prime wolf country.

Leading reindeer back to the Tsataan camp. The reindeer return to the vicinity of the camp each afternoon and as darkness falls they are led back into the camp and tethered overnight for safety.

Reindeer Riders

The Tsataan people are traditionally riders of reindeer so I was keen to persuade them to let me sit on the back of one of their animals. The reindeer bull did not move a muscle when I got up on to him bareback. Sitting close to his shoulder, away from the low point of the back, it felt a bit precarious. There was nothing really to hang on to, although the antlers were tempting! I think I would have needed practice from a very young age to master the art. The reindeer never flinched as I wriggled about, and I wondered how I would fare with riding one of ours at home. They were, after all, a similar size.

I sat on the reindeer bareback, but the Tsataan normally use saddles on their reindeer. The saddle itself, a wooden

The author riding a Mongolian reindeer bull belonging to the Tsataan – 'It felt like a balancing act and I was quite glad the reindeer didn't decide to move'.

frame set on thick blankets to protect the back, can be used on horses and reindeer, and can also be used for packing the reindeer. Although the Tsataan are small people, they still looked top heavy when perched on a reindeer's back.

It would, of course, be marvellous to return to these people at different times of year, perhaps to witness calving, summer life on the mountain tundra or the harshness of winter when the temperatures plummet to −35 °C! But Mongolia was a frustrating country in many respects; one minute you love it and the next minute you hate it. Mutton, milk and flour made up the staple diet, which is fine if you don't mind eating the same food every day. Time in Mongolia is also less clearly defined than at home. We spent many hours waiting for transport that was supposed to pick us up at a certain time, but in fact the driver had decided to wait to see if he could cram in any more passengers to make the journey worth his while. Jeep rides in Mongolia are like a never-ending rollercoaster ride, along roads that are a far cry from anything we would describe as a road at home. Fourteen days on horseback crippled my knees and not surprisingly left me with a pretty sore backside. But all the grief was outweighed by the fabulous scenery, incredibly hospitable people and very cheap vodka, and it was an honour to experience the Tsataan's humble way of life.

The Future for the Tsataan

There is no doubt that the Tsataan way of life is increasingly difficult to maintain, and it may be just a question of time before it becomes untenable. As a result of a delayed flight from Beijing to Ulanbataar, I met quite by chance an anthropologist called Hamid Sadar, who is studying the Tsataan and was himself on his way back out to visit some of them. He explained to me that traditionally the Tsataan find their food by hunting wild animals, fishing and gathering the fruits of the forest, their reindeer providing both a means to travel through the taiga and a source of rich milk. Sadly, however, the wealth of wildlife that used to roam the taiga is declining. The pressure of outsiders hunting for trophies, antlers and by-products like musk and velvet antler has decimated the populations of wildlife that the Tsataan traditionally hunt and eat. As a result they have had to turn to their own reindeer as a source of meat in times of need, and this has led to a steady decline in numbers over the last few decades. In 1977 there were more than 2,275 domesticated reindeer, but the 200 or so Tsataan left in Mongolia today now have only about 650 reindeer.

The People of the Lake

On our way to the Tsataan we chanced upon a reindeer family who visit the shores of Lake Khovsgol each year to cash in on the tourist interest in Mongolia's reindeer. They had been staying by the lake for the duration of the short tourist season in July and August, and as we passed through on horseback they were packing up to leave for the winter, returning to the north where all the other families lived. Although it was the end of the tourist season there was an air of general excitement and the male reindeer, packed with the people's belongings and ready to go, were surrounded by a throng of tourists taking photographs. The females and

All packed and ready to go at Lake Khovsgol, these reindeer are carrying their herders' worldly belongings.

calves were haltered and led by family members. Interestingly none of the reindeer was being ridden; instead Mongolian horses carried the humans.

Our guide Butsuuri explained that many tourists visit this family and their reindeer each summer, and they make a considerable amount of money from the tourists who want to take photographs. Unfortunately there is a downside to this enterprise, as a result of keeping these reindeer so low down in the summer months when they should really be up on the mountain tundra. Neither the climate nor the vegetation is suitable for them and they suffer severe health problems, with many of the young stock dying. But the family has become so rich that they merely go back to the taiga and buy more reindeer for the next year. The park authority that manages the area tries to discourage them from doing this but understandably these very poor people are reluctant to see the end of this very welcome form of revenue.

Hamid Sadar, the anthropologist I spoke to at Beijing airport, felt very strongly that the family should be banned from this practice. But I just wonder if there is some possibility of a compromise here. Our own experience with reindeer in general has shown that older, mature reindeer fare much better than young stock when they are kept away from their natural environment. Without a doubt tourists are keen to visit Mongolia's only reindeer and to a large extent the people beside Lake Khovsgol probably satisfy that demand. If they were encouraged to take only mature males and non-breeding females down to the lakeside for the summer, this would inevitably reduce the numbers of people wanting to visit the families in the taiga and the animals would not encounter the same health problems. Lake Khovsgol is increasingly popular as a tourist destination and demand is only going to rise in the future. Rather than unnecessarily disturb the Tsataan in their everyday lives up in the taiga, perhaps a honey pot drawing the majority of visitors to the shores of the lake would help to keep the pressure off those who are trying to lead traditional lives. And perhaps those tourist dollars could be redirected into research to help improve these people's lives and reverse the downward trend of reindeer families and their reindeer.

T E N

Exporting Reindeer to Other Lands

During the period of worldwide exploration and the discovery of new lands, the urge to introduce familiar animals to various places throughout the world was very prevalent. Very little thought, if any at all, was given to the impact these animals would have on the native fauna and flora. In some cases such introductions were entirely accidental.

Reindeer, because of their tractable nature, were obvious candidates for introduction into various arctic and sub-arctic areas, both mainland and islands. Some were even taken to the southern hemisphere, to the islands of South Georgia, Iles Kerguelen and Isla Navarino in sub-Antarctica. One of the earliest mentions of reindeer being sent overseas occurs in a book written in 1555 by Olaus Magnus. In *A Description of Northern Peoples* he describes the natural history of reindeer and their usefulness to man. He also mentions them being sent to foreign countries, especially overseas, but never surviving long. In particular he refers to six reindeer, accompanied by a married couple from Lapland, being sent to the Duke of Holstein. Sadly neither reindeer nor humans survived for long! Although a few, mainly unsuccessful, introductions were made during the eighteenth and nineteenth centuries to Iceland and Britain, the vast majority of the reindeer moves occurred during the early to middle of the twentieth century. Quite often the intention was to form the basis of a new industry for the native people in areas where they did not traditionally live by herding reindeer.

Small Island Irruptions and Crashes

Reindeer were introduced to more than thirty different locations during the twentieth century, particularly on remote arctic islands or areas restricted by glaciers. Here they were often left uncontrolled and were allowed to breed without restriction in the absence of humans or other predators. Some populations failed soon after their introduction; on Baffin Island, for example, the failure was blamed on the mistaken identification of sphagnum moss as reindeer lichen. On Great Cloche Island the reindeer quickly became infected with a parasite and died out.

However, when a small population of reindeer arrived on high-quality pristine summer grazing it was not uncommon for the herd numbers to increase exponentially in the early years, partly as a result of increased fertility among the female reindeer, in particular females who reached sexual maturity at just six months old and so had their first calf at a year old. One of the best-documented cases concerns St Matthew Island in the Bering Straits, where twenty-nine reindeer were introduced in 1944. Astonishingly this group multiplied rapidly and had grown to more than half a million in just twenty years. This rise was followed by a dramatic crash in numbers to almost zero in the next six years. Although the crash coincided with a number of severe winters, the harsh climate was not thought to be the only factor, since reindeer on adjacent islands did not suffer the same losses. As with other grazing populations, the effects of overgrazing can be dramatic, and this can be particularly accentuated with reindeer, which require very high-quality summer grazing to prepare for the ravages of winter. Once the population of St Matthew Island began to pressurise the summer grazing, the reindeer could not properly prepare for the winter and so considerable numbers died. The number of deaths was further increased by the destruction of slow-growing lichens that were integral to their survival over the winter months.

Different islands provided different ecological conditions for the introduced reindeer populations, and following an initial irruption in numbers some of the islands went on to

Reindeer on South Georgia, Antarctica. These introduced Norwegian reindeer are quite at home in South Georgia and have adapted to eat predominantly tussock grass.

reach an equilibrium between the numbers of reindeer and the carrying capacity of the grazing range, and to this day there are still reindeer on some of these islands.

One of the best-researched island populations of introduced reindeer is to be found on South Georgia, an island off mainland Antarctica. Brought in by Norwegian whalers on three separate occasions between 1911 and 1925, the reindeer provided a welcome respite from whale meat but also fulfilled a role as a sporting amenity. Their introduction followed in the wake of other animals introduced to serve the whaling community. Cows, sheep, goats and pigs were all brought in to supply meat and milk but they remained domesticated and never became feral. The rationale behind the reindeer introduction was that this was an animal that would require no time-consuming husbandry and management.

Some of the reindeer cows arrived heavy in calf, but of course the reversal of the seasons in the southern hemisphere meant that the calves were born at the beginning of winter and so perished. It took the reindeer two years to adapt to the change in seasons, with the associated reversal of rutting, calving, antler cycle and moulting. There were early losses due to avalanches of snow, but the reindeer appeared to thrive. Left to their own devices and basically uncontrolled, despite some culling for sport and meat, the reindeer quickly consumed all the available lichen and the tastiest summer plants. They then resorted to eating the dominant vegetation, *Poa flabellate*, a species of tussock grass available in both summer and winter. To this day tussock grass is the main diet of the reindeer on South Georgia, providing a rare example of a reindeer population that does not rely on lichens in winter to survive.

Today the reindeer here are separated into two genetically different herds by glaciers. There is considerable debate as to their long-term future on South Georgia, bearing in mind they are non-native and there is an international agreement to remove, in time, all non-native species from Antarctica. Early experiments in catching reindeer calves and taking them to the Falkland Islands for farming and tourism have been met with mixed success. Moreover, although the reindeer would be relatively easy to eradicate, the rats that were accidentally introduced on to the island will be much more difficult, and there is an argument that the more challenging non-native fauna and flora should be removed first. Almost a century on, this little herd of reindeer is now genetically distinct and they are thriving away from the Arctic, with its current problems, including radioactivity, pollution and diminishing habitat. Perhaps this is an argument strong enough to keep this healthy population on South Georgia.

Reindeer, Religion and Sharp Business Practice

The spread of Christianity across the world and the influence of missionaries on the daily lives and beliefs of indigenous peoples are well documented. Indeed, not even remote Inuit populations living on the arctic coastline of Alaska escaped religious interference to try and better their traditional lives.

The Inuit people of western Alaska were subsistence hunters who relied on a variety of prey to survive. They lived a relatively sedentary life on the arctic coastline for thousands of years, sustained by seals, whales, sea fish and the annually migrating caribou populations. Changes in the pattern of caribou migration meant that fewer caribou came by the Inuit settlements and this, combined with a shortage of whale meat after whaling ships from Europe and America arrived, resulted in starvation conditions for many of these indigenous people.

Desperate times need desperate measures and so a plan was put to the American Congress by the Revd Sheldon Jackson. He proposed that the Inuit should give up their unstable and unpredictable hunting way of life and instead become reindeer herders like the Chukchi, their neighbours across the Bering Straits in Russia, regardless of the fact that this was totally against the Inuit culture and traditional way of life.

Following reconnaissance trips to Siberia and early experiments with a small group of 16 domesticated reindeer that were shipped across the Bering Straits to the Unalaska

Islands, 171 reindeer were brought over from Siberia to mainland Alaska during the summer of 1892. With the reindeer came four Siberians who would teach the Inuit how to care for the animals. An early stumbling block was the fact that there was no love lost between Siberian reindeer herders and Inuit hunters, and fairly early on it became apparent that there would be little cooperation between the two. Indeed, the Siberians were soon replaced by Sami reindeer herders, who had been promised a better way of life than they endured at home in Lapland.

By 1902 a total of 1,200 reindeer had come from Russia, after which the Tsar of Russia closed the border, thus preventing any further exports. Sheldon Jackson hoped that reindeer herding would become the mainstay of the Inuit economy, and certainly the value of the reindeer was reinforced by the discovery of gold in the area. Not only would the reindeer provide meat for the Inuit, but they could also be put to work as beasts of burden hauling freight through the forests to the gold-mining communities.

The demand for draught reindeer was immense. Following orders from Congress, in 1897 a boatload of 538 castrated reindeer, already trained to pull sledges, was shipped across the Atlantic from Norway to New York, for onward transport by rail to Seattle and then by boat to Alaska. With the reindeer came 118 Sami herders and their families to teach the Alaskan native people the ways of reindeer herding. Copious supplies of lichen were brought along to keep the reindeer on their accustomed diet for the duration of the voyage across the Atlantic. The Lapps cared for the reindeer diligently, and only one reindeer died during the crossing and that was due to injuries sustained in a fight. Once disembarked on the American mainland, the reindeer were transported by train to Seattle. But here disaster struck. The lichen supply had all but run out and in a desperate attempt to save supplies for the onward journey to Alaska, they took the reindeer to graze in the local city park. This had dire consequences. Reindeer do not adapt well to sudden changes of diet and that night several of the reindeer died. Things then went from bad to worse, and by the time the reindeer reached their final destination in Alaska there were only 144 survivors.

Sheldon Jackson's intention was that the reindeer should ultimately become the property of the native people, providing them with income and food. Over the first 15 years the reindeer numbers increased sevenfold to more than 10,000, some 2,700 of which were owned by at least 60 Inuit. The project was set up in such a way that the Inuit apprentices 'earned' their reindeer. During training, Inuit who stayed the course were loaned two female reindeer each year. The offspring of those females became their own personal property. More reindeer stations were built and the reindeer population continued to increase. The cultural impact of young Inuit hunters turning herders was immense, but as long as the reindeer could be kept close to settlements all year round there was little effect on their sedentary lifestyle. However, as the numbers of reindeer grew the grazing areas close to the stations became overgrazed and the Inuit had to adopt nomadic ways of reindeer herding, moving with the herds to find winter lichen pastures and taking them to fresh summer grazing on the coast. This led to problems as the Inuit were reluctant to pursue what was clearly a very different way of life on the move.

Nevertheless, the Alaskan reindeer industry expanded quickly. Despite Jackson's noble intentions, commercial exploitation and non-native ownership of the herds increased. In particular the Lappish families that had stayed in Alaska were treated far better than the Inuit when it came to reindeer ownership. This preferential treatment and their good reindeer husbandry led to a number of Lapp reindeer herders accumulating relatively large herds of their own. By 1920 over half of the 300,000 domesticated reindeer were owned by non-natives.

Notorious among the private non-native owners were the Lomen brothers, who arrived in Nome, Alaska, in 1900 to make their fortunes from gold mining. Their interest was sparked when 1,200 reindeer owned by Lapp Alfred Nilima were offered for sale. Despite the plans for only natives to own reindeer, the government did not object to the sale of reindeer between non-natives, a decision which left many Inuit disillusioned. While the government struggled to find the best management practice for native-owned herds,

Alaskan reindeer gathered for slaughter, Kotzebue, 1915.

Lomen and Company forged ahead with expanding herd numbers and proposals to export reindeer meat and associated products. 'Natural freezers' were built in the permafrost, with a total capacity of 10,000 carcasses, with adjacent corrals, slaughterhouses and processing units. Easy access for shipping completed the picture, which saw huge quantities of reindeer meat being shipped to mainland America. Between 1928 and 1930 the Lomens shipped some 30,000 reindeer carcasses along with thousands of reindeer skins for making gloves. The Lomen brothers had cornered the market and their ever-increasing herds of reindeer competed for grazing with the native-owned herds. Conflict was inevitable, and accentuated by the sharp business practices they adopted. An 'open herd system' was introduced, whereby the Inuit herds were mixed with the non-native herds; inevitably the Inuit herding practices were thrown into disarray and they suffered considerable losses.

The protests from natives regarding the Lomen brothers' activities fell on deaf ears in government. Indeed the government agents in Alaska were all too often influenced by the powerful Lomen brothers, who now largely controlled the reindeer-herding industry. Moreover, Judge G.J. Lomen presided over the district court and so the family also dominated the local legal establishment. It wasn't until 1933 that the protests of the natives were finally heard and following a confidential report it was recommended that the Lomen Corporation should cease trading. By 1934 the Lomen brothers had conceded that there was no future for them in Alaska and that reindeer herding should be handed over to the natives. Congress provided funds to implement the Reindeer Act, which allowed for the compulsory purchase of all non-native herds and facilities and their redistribution to native owners. Fifty years on and the American government had finally legislated in favour of the natives, who would now enjoy sole ownership of the reindeer that had been brought in specifically to better their lives.

Up until the mid-1970s the reindeer, which were largely confined to the Seward peninsula, generated substantial income for the rural Alaskan community in the production of reindeer meat and velvet antler. The Seward peninsula had traditionally been an area devoid of wild caribou, but between 1976 and 1996 the Western Arctic Caribou Herd increased in size from 75,000 to 463,000, spreading west as it grew into the Seward peninsula. Historically in Russia, Canada and Greenland it has not been possible for domesticated and wild reindeer to co-exist because of the problems of the wild herds 'stealing' the domesticated animals. Reindeer herders lost anything between 75 and 100 per cent of their reindeer, and over 12,000 animals went to join the wild caribou herds. Regular contact with their reindeer was lost and many reindeer herders fell by the wayside. Recent efforts to re-establish the industry have begun in a sporadic fashion, but as long there are wild caribou stealing the reindeer it will be a very difficult job.

The Great Trek

In 1926 the Canadian government commissioned a survey of the western Arctic with a view to finding a suitable site to establish reindeer herding for the Inuit in arctic Canada. Two Danish botanists were hired and their final report recommended the Mackenzie River delta as the most suitable site.

Once again it was the Lomen brothers who benefited most from the subsequent deal, which entailed the sale of 3,000 reindeer. These would be herded overland from Alaska, covering some 1,600 miles of uncharted terrain. The Lomen brothers hired the expert Andy Bahr, a Laplander who had come over to America with the original boatload of reindeer destined to work in the gold mines. Although retired and now 63 years of age, Bahr took up the challenge of taking the reindeer to Canada. It was estimated that the trek would take two years, and the route would go inland across the Brook range of the Rocky Mountains to avoid the herds of caribou on the arctic coast.

So it was that on Boxing Day 1929 the herd of reindeer, accompanied by loaded dog sleds, reindeer sleds, Laplanders and Inuits, set out from Kotzebue Sound on the Alaskan coast. The trek was fraught with problems, including atrocious weather, predators, biting insects and passing caribou stealing reindeer. At times conditions forced a change in route. Two years eventually became five years, but finally 2,375 reindeer arrived at their destination; only 10 per cent of them were the original animals that set off on the trek.

These reindeer became the basis of the Canadian Reindeer Project, which for three decades was based at Reindeer Station on the east branch of the Mackenzie River and supplied reindeer meat for the region. The government project was eventually discontinued and the herd was privatised in the 1960s. It has changed hands several times and is currently owned by the Kuek Resource Development Corporation, better known as 'Canadian Reindeer', a private company based in Inuvik. The income from approximately 5,000 reindeer is generated from meat, tourism and live sales.

Pollyanna and the Submarine

One of the most bizarre stories of reindeer on the move must be the account of a young reindeer living in a submarine during the Second World War. The tale begins in the Russian port of Polyarnoe, situated just downstream from Murmansk on the Kola peninsula. HMS *Trident* docked at Polyarnoe during the war with engine troubles, and the commanding officer, Commander Geoffrey Sladen DSO, DSC, was invited to dine with the Port Admiral. Over the course of dinner, inspired by the amount of snow lying about, Commander Sladen spoke about the problems his young wife faced pushing their baby's pram up the steep hill to their house in snowy conditions. The Port Admiral suggested that what she needed was a reindeer.

A few days went by and nothing more was said, but just before the submarine shipped out to sea once more a reindeer arrived on the dockside, accompanied by a barrel of freshly picked lichen. Unwilling to 'look a gift reindeer in the mouth', Commander Sladen agreed to the animal coming on board. This was by no means an easy feat, as the reindeer wriggled and squirmed as they manoeuvred her down through the narrow torpedo-loading hatch, which had a diameter of just 21in.

Petty Officer James Riddoch was instructed to look after the 'gift'. He commented later that he had been on many courses during his time with the Navy but never had the topic of livestock care been covered. He had to judge for himself how much lichen the young reindeer should get each day and what other food they might be able to feed her. Naturally he soon won the nickname 'zoo attendant'.

On leaving Polyarnoe HMS *Trident* rounded the North Cape of Norway to be met by hurricane-force gales. It was a particularly rough passage, and the reindeer sought refuge in the officers' toilets. However, the pitching and rolling of the submarine did not affect her appetite and she was soon causing chaos by trotting through the narrow gangways in search of the barrel of lichen.

A week into their voyage home, HMS *Trident* received orders from the Admiralty to stay on patrol as German warships were in the vicinity. As the days passed, the young reindeer began to acclimatise to her new home, always finding her way to the control room at the time when the main hatch was opened and fresh air poured in. She would stand with her front feet high on the ladder, taking in deep breaths of fresh air. When the conning tower was shut, the increasing staleness of the air often caused the reindeer to pant. A bigger problem, though, was that her lichen supply was dangerously low and would very soon run out. There was much discussion among the crew as to what they might feed her. However, she solved the problem for them by making her way past the officers' kitchen to help herself to leftovers from the waste buckets. In particular, she developed a taste for diluted condensed milk. Indeed, the little reindeer settled in well to life in the submarine, taking up residence in the captain's cabin when the submarine was submerged and heading for the main hatch for fresh air whenever it surfaced. She seemed to enjoy her life under the

Pollyanna with Commander Sladen at the dockside in Blyth after her weeks at sea.

ocean waves, but the crew weren't quite so sure. She had developed a pungent odour that, added to the normal smells in the submarine, made life almost unbearable when they were submerged for long periods.

A whole month passed, during which time the reindeer encountered plenty of wartime action, including the successful attack on the German heavy cruiser *Prinz Eugen*. When the submarine eventually arrived at Blyth in Northumberland, the reindeer (now known as 'The Goat' by the crew) had put on weight and her antlers had grown so much that they had to saw off the tips to get her back out through the hatch. To assist her exit from the submarine, they inserted her into a large canvas bag. Once on land she sprang out of the bag and legged it along the jetty with the *Trident*'s crew and dock workers in hot pursuit. She was finally caught and led off to naval headquarters. She was named Pollyanna by the naval authorities at Blyth and eventually was presented to London Zoo, where she became quite a character. It was rumoured that whenever she heard bells or anything that sounded like the submarine's tannoy, she would lower her head as though she was preparing for diving stations!

ELEVEN

Scotland's Reindeer Herd

At the tail end of the period when reindeer were being moved to various points around the world, a proposal was put to Britain's Ministry of Agriculture in the late 1940s to reintroduce reindeer to Scotland. Dr Lindgren, a social anthropologist, and her new husband, Sami reindeer herder Mikel Utsi, were the driving force behind this suggestion. Mr Utsi was an expert reindeer herder and Dr Lindgren had all the diplomatic skills required to woo the authorities in the British government. Better still, this formidable team was privately financed. Having gained approval for their plans, they searched for the best place in the Scottish Highlands to bring the reindeer to, and then devoted the latter halves of their lives to the project's success.

Wedding Vows and Reindeer

Married late in life, Mr Utsi and Dr Lindgren were an extraordinary couple. Mikel Utsi was Sami, spoke only broken English and stood just 5ft 4in tall. Dr Ethel John Lindgren was the daughter of a Swedish-American banker, she had studied Chinese and Anthropology at Cambridge University, spoke at least five languages fluently, had taken part in expeditions to the Tungus in Manchuria during the early 1920s and stood over 6ft tall. The couple met while Dr Lindgren was in Swedish Lapland studying the Sami people. Perhaps she felt her only chance of persuading Mr Utsi to get married and come and live with her in Britain was to promise that he could bring his herd of reindeer with him!

When Mr Utsi visited the Scottish Highlands at the end of the 1940s he was struck by the similarities between the Scottish landscape and habitat and his own reindeer-grazing lands in north Sweden. He was convinced, quite rightly as it turned out, that reindeer could do well in this new land, especially since they had lived here perhaps as recently as 800 years ago, and Scotland offered a habitat very similar to their homeland Lapland. Another part of the argument for the project played on the fact that food rationing was still in place in Britain after the Second World War and the reindeer would provide a very welcome source of meat.

In *The Orkneyinga* saga it is written that the Vikings hunted reindeer and red deer in Caithness and Sutherland. Certainly they would have known the difference between the two species as both are native to Scandinavia. However, there is no archaeological evidence to substantiate this claim. Perhaps the Vikings themselves brought the reindeer across – a not unlikely suggestion since reindeer were certainly domesticated by the Viking era. The last evidence for wild reindeer in Great Britain dates to what was probably an interglacial phase some 3,000 or 4,000 years ago.

The First Reindeer

So it was that in 1952 the first small consignment of eight reindeer was taken by boat from Sweden via Narvik in Norway to Scotland. There were 2 bulls, 1 castrated male (ox), 2 young females and 3 female calves. They arrived at Rothesay dock, Clydebank, on 12 April 1952, and were transported immediately into quarantine for 28 days at the Royal Zoological Society in Edinburgh. Sarek the ox seemed rather an unnecessary addition to a breeding group, but Mr Utsi was hoping to do more than just bring reindeer back to Scotland – he was also bringing his Sami culture, in which castrated males play an important part. In fact Sarek, with his bell round his neck, was the herd leader and the pack animal, and if Mr Utsi hadn't been sentimental then Sarek would have been the first reindeer to be eaten. Instead Sarek went on to lead the herd for many years, dying eventually at the grand old age of 16 years.

Sarek, with antlers, and his young companion in quarantine before being released into their new home in the Scottish Highlands.

Subsequent consignments were brought in over the next couple of years, with the third consignment causing a considerable stir among the authorities when Mr Utsi decided to bring one more animal than had been permitted, in his words 'to cover any losses that may occur en route'. It took all Dr Lindgren's diplomatic skills to smooth the waves following a formal letter of protest from the Ministry of Agriculture at Tolworth.

The reindeer brought in during the early years were kept on low ground on the Rothiemurchus Estate, beside Aviemore. The late Colonel Grant, intrigued by the project, provided them with a few hundred acres of land and a cottage at Moormore, on the Rothiemurchus Estate, for the herder. There were problems with the low ground and without a doubt from the very start Mr Utsi had his eye on the Cairngorm Mountains that dominated the landscape to the south of Moormore. By 1954 Dr Lindgren and Mr Utsi had persuaded the Forestry Commission for Scotland to let them move their modest herd of reindeer up on to the northern slopes of the Cairngorms. Some 6,000 acres of open moor land, rising to 4,000ft, were soon made available to the reindeer. This move to higher ground, where the cool breeze kept the flies away in the summer and the vegetation all year round was more appropriate, was a turning point for the herd and really set the project on a new footing.

Early Interest in the Herd

The reindeer inevitably attracted a lot of attention from various quarters. The general public, amused by the prospect of Santa's reindeer being resident in Britain, were made welcome and from very early on Mr Utsi proudly showed visitors his beloved reindeer. Often dressed in traditional Sami costume, he caused quite a stir and many people remembered the charismatic Mr Utsi more than the reindeer themselves. A visit in the spring of 1953 from an ill-informed SSPCA officer resulted in a complaint being sent to the Department of Agriculture, alleging neglect of the reindeer. What the officer didn't appreciate was that he had visited the reindeer when they were in full moult. The moulting of the light-coloured winter coat contrasting with the short dark summer coat underneath make even reindeer in the finest condition look particularly moth-eaten. A subsequent report by the Department of Agriculture completely vindicated Mr Utsi, but it made him think twice about taking visitors to see the reindeer when they were moulting.

In the hope of finding cheap meat supplies for his company's tinned dog foods, a representative from Chappie Ltd visited the herd and offered Mr Utsi 6*d* per pound for any surplus reindeer meat. Certainly one of the primary aims of establishing reindeer in Scotland was to provide meat, but not dog meat, and in Mr Utsi's words the Chappie rep was 'shown the door'.

The early years on virgin ground were challenging times for Mr Utsi and the herd grew slowly. By March 1956 the herd total was twelve and the subsequent calving produced another four calves. Early losses through accidents, dog worrying and straying were devastating at the time, but they merely set the project back. Mr Utsi's zeal and determination kept the experiment on track and by the end of the 1950s the herd was going from strength to strength.

Mr Utsi's Helpers

Although Mr Utsi spent a lot of time in Scotland with the reindeer he did not live there permanently and in his absence he depended on assistants to care for the reindeer. His expectations were very high and he demanded 110 per cent effort from all his volunteers and employees. He was certainly a difficult man to please and many people felt unable to keep up with his demands. On one particular

Reindeer at Moormore, Rothiemurchus. For the first few years the reindeer were kept on low ground on the Rothiemurchus Estate, but it was only a question of time before Mr Utsi gained permission to take his reindeer to higher ground.

occasion two volunteers out looking for stray reindeer ended up accidentally letting go of their two reindeer, still with their halters on and ropes trailing. Mr Utsi was furious and sent them back out to find the reindeer with the trailing ropes. When they returned without the precious reindeer, Mr Utsi drove them straight to the train station in Aviemore and put them on the next train south.

The original reindeer brought in from Sweden had a tendency to stray. They had come from migrating herds of reindeer and so their urge to move with the seasons was

strong. Much of the work involved gathering up these strays from all around the Cairngorms and bringing them back to base. Neighbouring sporting estates, conscious of the foreigners in the hills, were regularly asked to look out for strays. One gamekeeper, approached to see if he had seen any reindeer, asked if there had been any interbreeding with red deer, 'because I have seen a deer with a very odd-shaped pair of antlers'. There were also reports of 'ghost reindeer' in Glen Feshie on the west side of the Cairngorm range, but Mr Utsi put this down to 'a few too many tots of whisky'.

Mr Utsi with his pioneer reindeer on the northern slopes of the Cairngorms.
This set the project on a whole new footing.

Volunteer reindeer herders came from all walks of life, from local lads to university students. Their accommodation moved from Moormore Cottage on the Rothiemurchus Estate to Reindeer House, a substantial bungalow built by Dr Lindgren and Mr Utsi in Glenmore in 1960. Commanding a fine position in the Glenmore Forest and with a clear view of the northern slopes of the Cairngorms, Reindeer House was ideally positioned for the keepers to watch the reindeer on the hill. Reindeer House was very much regarded as a place of work rather than a home, and Mr Utsi was very specific about the fixtures, fittings and general decor. There were no comfortable sofas or settees and the only source of heat was a small coal fire. Apparently he believed that if he provided the workers with too much comfort they would become lazy and stay in the house. It is perhaps not surprising that over a period of thirty years Mr Utsi saw more than 500 staff, both paid and voluntary, come and go.

By the mid-1970s Mr Utsi's health was failing and he was no longer able to walk up into the hills to see his beloved reindeer. Frustrated by illness, he had to depend more and more on his assistants to look after the herd. The hot summer of 1976 took its toll on the herd, but Mr Utsi, depressed by the losses, blamed the keepers. His journeys north to Glenmore became less frequent and the demoralised workforce did their best to keep tabs on the reindeer. By the autumn of 1978 Dr Lindgren was once again looking for new staff to tend the herd on the hill. An advert was placed in the local Highland paper, the *Press and Journal*, for a reindeer keeper. A school-leaver from Caithness answered the advert, and following a short interview was offered the job. Alan Smith had no idea what to expect; as the son of a hill farmer/deer stalker he imagined himself driving a tractor and

Reindeer-keeper Alan Smith with Dimitri. It was to be a steep learning curve for school-leaver Alan after Mr Utsi's death in the summer of 1979.

trailer and feeding the beasts hay and silage. He could not have been more wrong! In fact his back yard was the Cairngorm massif, Britain's largest arctic plateau area, and the only means of access was on foot. Luckily for Mr Utsi, Alan had been brought up in the hills and was quite unfazed by the prospect of tramping the hills looking for reindeer. Within days of arriving he spotted some reindeer about 4 miles away, grazing on the far skyline. He phoned Mr Utsi with the news that he had located part of the herd, only to be told, 'You must have a good pair of binoculars.' Mr Utsi never made it north in the last year of his life and so Alan was very much left to his own devices. Although daily diaries had always been kept, there was no hands-on expertise to be handed down and from day one Alan had to learn the ropes the hard way. Mr Utsi died the following June in Cambridge and with his death a tremendous amount of knowledge was lost forever. Alan was Mr Utsi's last reindeer keeper, and twenty-seven years on he is still in charge.

Scottish Reindeer Herding

The fifty-plus years of life in the Cairngorms have produced a unique herd of reindeer. They do not thrive as captive animals, since captivity means they have to be looked after completely artificially, with neither their diet nor their surroundings bearing any resemblance to their natural life. As highly specialised arctic and sub-arctic animals, they need a wide selection of plant material to feed on, preferably with lichen for winter feed (although as we have seen, lichen is not a necessity for all naturally occurring reindeer). Essential or not, it certainly puts a smile on a reindeer's face. Our management of the reindeer today is a balancing act between allowing them to free range and live a natural life, and the need to enclose at least part of the herd, particularly in the summer months, so that we have a base that we can retrieve reindeer to and also can guarantee there will be reindeer for the visitors to see.

The Cairngorms have been home to the reindeer since 1952, but when Alan and I took over the ownership of the herd in 1989 we quickly decided that we should move part of the herd to a new site. Thus since 1990 part of the herd has lived at our second site on the Crown Estate at Glenlivet. This was another turning point for the herd, which had always struggled to increase in numbers on the Cairngorms alone. Reduced grazing pressure on the original site and the availability of fresh grazing and undisturbed pastures at Glenlivet meant that the herd numbers grew during the following years and now we have about 150 animals in all.

From the beginning Mr Utsi named all his reindeer and gave them individual ear tags to help the volunteers and staff identify them. These, combined with distinctive traits such as colour, antler shape and character, allow the reindeer to be identified relatively easily. Even today, the herd is very much regarded as a group of individuals. Each year the new-born calves are named after a particular theme, such as trees, mountains, colours and Scottish towns. The most difficult time to tell the reindeer apart is when their antlers have fallen off, because antler shape is peculiar to each individual and each year when the antlers regrow the same basic shape is repeated. To this day the naming of our reindeer is an integral part of the work, and at the end of the summer, when we know what our calf numbers are, we set about the task of finding a theme and assigning each calf a name.

The Cairngorm reindeer are basically a sedentary herd with a short seasonal movement up on to the higher ground of the Cairngorms in the summer months. They come off the high plateau at the end of the summer, although this is not to seek shelter but to find food still growing lower down. Although they visit the forest margin in search of food, they do not need to seek shelter like the native red deer, which lack the quality of coat that the reindeer have. Always on the move, the reindeer have very little impact on the composition of vegetation and can even be beneficial. The northern corries of the Cairngorms, for example, where the reindeer are most often seen, have seen the regeneration of native Caledonian pine trees. This is because unlike red deer and sheep, reindeer do not browse

Alan with the herd today, twenty-seven years after he first started working with it.

on Scots Pine trees or strip the bark. Reindeer have very delicate dentition, which has an interesting effect on their browsing technique for deciduous trees like birch and willow. Where red deer and sheep will bite off the whole growing shoot when browsing deciduous trees, reindeer in contrast merely strip the leaves, in effect plucking them from the growing shoot. I think this may be the fundamental difference between the impact of red deer and reindeer on regenerating woodland. Further evidence is to be found in the wealth of regenerating woodland in Scandinavia and Russia, where wild and domesticated reindeer are naturally found. Indeed, reindeer would in general be a much better herbivore to live on the high ground of Scotland, as they are able to withstand the rigours of winter on the high ground and can live more in harmony with the natural vegetation.

So what is the future for Britain's only naturally occurring herd of reindeer. Since 1952 the herd has undergone a number of important phases, from the original import to the consolidation of the herd in the 1970s, which helped the animals to recover from the hot summer of 1976. As Mr Utsi's health failed his keepers struggled to emulate his expertise but over time more and more experience was gained and today the herd's future has been secured with a mix of traditional and new methods of management. Mr Utsi always said he wanted to leave the reindeer to be looked after by the Scottish people. That has happened, and I think both he and Dr Lindgren would be proud of what has been achieved. So where does the herd go from here? Perhaps new land could be acquired to establish part of the herd at a third site in Scotland. Careful thought would have to go in to such a move, and doubtless Mr Utsi with all his knowledge picked a very good site in the 1950s. But this is very much a goal that we would like to achieve in our lifetime. Watch this space!

Modern-day Lapland

As I sat on the east side of Lake Akkajaure in Swedish Lapland and gazed across the water to Sarek National Park and the summer grazing for many Swedish mountain reindeer, I could understand why Mikel Utsi had taken reindeer from his homeland in arctic Sweden to the Cairngorm Mountains in the Highlands of Scotland. The two landscapes are remarkably alike. We were there to meet up with Jussa Utsi, one of the late Mikel Utsi's nephews, who was going to take us by boat to his summer dwelling across the lake. We weren't quite sure what to expect but we had come laden with Scottish hospitality in the form of malt whisky, as this always seemed to go down well.

Summer in the Mountains

The weather was fantastic: a brilliant blue sky, not a breath of wind, the surface of the lake like a millpond and the sun high in the sky. We could have been on the Costa del Sol. Swedish Lapland, however, was a much better choice as far as I was concerned. When Jussa arrived he seemed to be in no hurry to get over the water, despite the fact that it was quite late in the day. But then, this was the season of the midnight sun and the sun would remain high in the sky all day and all night. We had timed our visit perfectly. Jussa was going to his summer camp, Vaisaluotka, that day and would stay there for the next ten weeks. Close and extended family would join him during that time to help with reindeer calf marking, fishing, moose hunting and finally

There are striking similarities between landscape and vegetation in Swedish Lapland (above) and the Cairngorm Mountains, Scotland (below).

the reindeer bull slaughter in the autumn before the rutting season, when the bulls would lose their condition in pursuit of the cows.

While we sat waiting for Jussa to gather all his belongings, a steady stream of helicopters were landing and taking off. Their passengers were reindeer herders, who, like Jussa, were going out to more remote settlements in the mountains. Being a helicopter pilot looked like a pretty lucrative business in north Sweden. Today's reindeer herders relied heavily on helicopters, snowmobiles and scrambler motorbikes – a far cry from reindeer sledges and the packed reindeer of yesteryear.

The lake we crossed in Jussa's boat was a flooded river valley, part of a massive hydroelectric scheme that destroyed vast areas of valuable reindeer grazing when the valley was originally dammed. Jussa, along with many Sami, was very bitter about the impact the hydroelectric scheme had had on their lives. They received no compensation for the loss of grazing and benefited little from the electricity generated, which was primarily to meet the demand from urban areas further south.

As we crossed the lake and approached the far shore, we could see all along the shoreline small isolated family encampments nestled in the dense birch woodland. Each family had its own little cluster of buildings, with winding paths and raised wooden walkways across boggy areas linking the communities. Depending on the water level in the lake, which was governed by the engineers operating the dams, the unloading of the boat was a greater or lesser chore. The ugly eroded shoreline all the way round indicated that the level was low, so we had to carry the luggage that much further. Jussa, who had no time for the hydroelectric companies, begrudged *any* carrying between boat and dwelling, and recalled that on three occasions his family had had to move their houses on to higher ground to prevent them flooding as the water levels rose.

Before we left for Vaisaluokta we had been warned by a number of people about the ferocity of the mosquitoes, the 'Sami army' as Jussa described them. Luckily the hot dry day and high-speed boat ride had kept them at bay . However, as the day cooled the mosquitoes became more evident and we were very glad of the mosquito screens across the windows. When we asked Jussa about the mosquitoes, he extolled their virtues. 'Mosquitoes,' he said, 'are the reindeer herders' best friend. Biting mosquitoes help to keep the reindeer together, which helps us to both locate the herds and gather them into the corrals for calf marking.' He added that they also keep the tourist population away, leaving the mountains undisturbed for the reindeer to graze in the summer.

That night we dined on smoked arctic char, freshly caught in the lake and cooked over a smoky fire, dried reindeer meat and freshly baked bread. The reindeer meat came in the form of a whole shoulder, still on the bone, which had been salted and dried. All Sami carry a sharp knife, which they use to cut off slices of meat.

Reminiscing

During the evening Jussa had been preparing his wood-fired sauna out in the washroom. Reached by a wooden walkway, which interconnected all the buildings because underfoot was so wet and boggy, the washroom was a wooden shed with a wooden slatted floor. The sauna occupied one corner, while the rest was set aside for washing clothes. There was an enormous vat of water heated by a wooden stove, and a mangle.

After a friendly communal sauna, the evening progressed to a fairly serious consumption of the whisky and by 3 a.m. we were all well under the influence of alcohol, despite the fact that it was still broad daylight. Embarrassingly, our Swedish was non-existent, although Jussa's English seemed to improve with every dram.

The life of Swedish Sami had changed dramatically over Jussa's lifetime. He remembered as a child travelling with herds of reindeer in spring on sledges pulled by reindeer as they moved many miles from their winter grazing in the forest to summer in the mountains. The journey took many weeks, with some cows calving on the way. The whole family made the journey, the fit and able on skis, the very young and the old travelling in sledges. Today the reindeer still migrate but the herds are guided by a few Sami on snowmobiles. The journey time is much shorter and fewer people are involved. When asked if he yearned for the traditional ways, Jussa answered emphatically, 'Life was very hard then,' he said. 'Modern-day reindeer herding is better for everyone.' We gathered that the life of a Sami reindeer herder is not dissimilar to that of a Scottish hill farmer, where alternative sources of income are crucial in order to survive. Sami families are unable to live by reindeer herding alone these days, and many of them have part-time work and their wives also go out to work. There is less interest among the younger generation, who seem reluctant to take on a business that involves a whole way of life and leaves them with little money and less leisure time. Such sentiments are echoed in farming communities at home in Scotland.

Mountain Corrals

Getting up after a night of over-indulgence is always tricky but we had only a limited time to spend at Vaisaluotka and we wanted to get an idea of the summer grazing range. So in the late morning we carefully headed up on to the ridge behind the Utsi encampment. As we climbed up through the trees along a well-worn path we were impressed by the wealth of growth. After a winter shrouded in snow and ice, the lengthening days gave the vegetation ample opportunity to grow at an amazing rate. As we gained height we noticed that the tree layer continued to grow profusely, but in a more shrub-like form. In fact, the shrubbery was so dense that it was almost impossible to walk off the path. We could understand how the reindeer here were able to grow so quickly over the short growing season, laying down sufficient fat reserves to last them through the lean winter months.

Our walk took us on to the ridge, where there were several permanent corrals with long guide fences radiating away from them. This was where the reindeer were gathered for the bull slaughter in the autumn, before being moved down off the mountains for the autumn rut and winter in the forests. Remnants of previous years' activities abounded: bones, skulls and antlers and even the odd beer tin littered the area. The corrals were pretty makeshift, formed out of thin poles, bleached by years of winter storms, and dishevelled wire netting. Each year cursory patching took place to keep the fences intact, but no new fencing had been erected for a long time. Although there were no reindeer close by, with binoculars we could see groups of a few hundred gathered together on the snowfields. In the heat of the day this was a good way for the reindeer to cool off and avoid being bitten by mosquitoes.

When we returned, Jussa was at the side of the lake talking on his mobile phone. He had a helicopter delivery organised and he was down there waiting for its imminent arrival. As the helicopter flew towards us over the lake, we could see something dangling below it. The cargo turned out to be two scrambler bikes that would be used in the mountains to gather the reindeer for calf marking in a few days' time. Unfortunately our time was short, so we could not stay for that. Luckily, though, on our way up to Vaisaluotka we had been able to visit two calf markings in forest regions further south.

Marking the Calves

Our first experience of calf marking was at a site near Arvidsjaur. Our guide and contact was a Swedish professor of reindeer husbandry, who was particularly interested in comparing the growth rates of different populations of reindeer in relation to climate and vegetation. We arrived in Arvidsjaur at about midday and went straight to the house of one of the Sami elders, who was organising the catch that day. We were told to go and find somewhere to stay for the night and they would call us once they had got the herd in. I suspect we would have been more of a hindrance than a help when it came to the tricky task of getting reindeer into a corral from the surrounding forest. The day was wearing on, so, having found suitable accommodation, we headed into town for supper. Back at our sleeping quarters for the night, we reckoned that since it was getting late, they must have been unsuccessful in rounding up the reindeer and the event would be postponed to another day. But we were wrong! A short time later the phone rang and we were told it was 'action stations'. The reindeer had been corralled and we should go immediately to the site.

The sight that met our eyes was almost unbelievable, and the noise was deafening. In the midst of a continuous coniferous forest was a corral the size of a football pitch, made up of propped-up wire netting and hessian. Inside this makeshift fence were at least 3,000 reindeer, all trotting round, the cows and calves constantly grunting to one another. It was mid-summer so all the adults were growing their new velvet antlers, and the bulls' antlers were distinctly longer than those of the cows. They were all still in full winter coat. In the midst of this moving mass of reindeer numerous people stood around looking intently at the reindeer. Each calf had to be individually identified by correctly reading its mother's ear notches. This was no mean feat when you consider that any individual may have as many as four or five different notches in each ear to determine ownership. In addition, reindeer ears are not very big and are extremely hairy, and the reindeer were constantly on the move. Once a calf was matched to a mother it would be caught by the back leg, using a sliding loop on the end of a long pole. Then a knife was used to cut ear notches identical to the mother's before the calf was released back into the group. A piece of ear from each calf was kept to count the calves marked at the end of the night's work. The constant grunting was mostly generated by mothers and calves desperately trying to relocate each other in the swirling mass of beasts. The reindeer constantly moved in one direction, anti-clockwise. The herders told us that the reindeer would only go clockwise when they were panicking, which might result in a stampede out of the makeshift corral. As long as the reindeer moved anti-clockwise they were calm and there was no problem.

Inevitably this process was very slow and with over a thousand calves to mark it was going to take hours. By about 4 a.m. the majority of the calves had been marked. Towards the end the people with the long sticks systematically caught the last few unmarked calves and hung a large number round each one's neck, then nearly everyone left the corrals and sat round open fires drinking tea and eating dried reindeer meat while the reindeer settled. A couple of men were left with the reindeer, writing down the calf numbers and trying to match them to their mothers. Then the catchers returned, caught the numbered calves and cut the corresponding notches in their ears. By 7 a.m. the last of the calves was marked, and the whole group was released back into the forest. The reindeer could finally relax and everyone could get some sleep. Later that morning we went back to the catch-up site. Trampled ground, a few small pieces of calves' ears and a couple of reindeer aimlessly wandering around was all that was left from the frenetic activity of the night before.

We then headed north-east to the town of Boden to meet up with another Sami, Agneta Mikaelson, who would take us to our next calf marking. After tea at her flat in Boden, Agneta led us at breakneck speed to the middle of another massive forest to meet her people, who were that night hoping to gather their reindeer. I don't think I had ever been driven so fast for so long on such a rough bumpy road in such a wholly inappropriate small family car. Rally driver Agneta was obviously keen we shouldn't miss the night's events.

Agneta is a fascinating lady. Her parents were both Sami, but in the area they lived in they had not been allowed to practise reindeer herding officially. In the past the Swedish government had banned reindeer herding in areas designated as outside Lapland and as a result a lot of their history had been all but lost. Agneta was researching the archives and gleaning evidence from Sami people to put her family and other Sami groups in the area 'back on the map'. Although Agneta lived in a town flat and did not work with the reindeer every day, she was still very proud to be Sami.

In contrast to the journey, when we arrived at our destination there seemed to be no hurry and we were treated to a marvellous feast of smoked reindeer meat sliced very thinly and fried before being heaped into pitta breads. While we ate we learned that the helicopter was already out in the forest, which stretched for miles and miles in every direction, bringing in the reindeer. It seemed inconceivable that in this vast area of forest, reindeer could be located and driven into a corral that was no bigger than a decent-sized garden.

Evidently the Sami knew their business, and before long it was apparent that the reindeer were approaching the corral with the helicopter guiding them in. It was already 10 p.m., so it was going to be another late night. The calf marking at Rodingsträsk was on a much smaller scale but the calves were individually caught and marked in just the same way. It was very much a family affair, with the youngest member, just 2 years old, as much in the thick of the activity as the adults. Not used to all this night-time activity, we departed before the end of the process, but we were there long enough to watch the sun set and rise again, in the same place and in the space of just a couple of minutes, with no marked change

Calf marking in the middle of the night; the long stick has a noose on the end for catching the calves.

in light intensity. It could have been the middle of the day, except my body clock was telling me I needed sleep. I imagine the Sami look forward to the long winter nights, when they can catch up on their sleep.

In hindsight, it was of course the obvious time of day to handle the reindeer. Although the sun still shone, it was much lower in the sky at night and so much cooler. Reindeer at the end of June are still in full winter coat so any handling during the heat of the day would have undoubtedly caused them stress. Also the mosquitoes were much less active in the middle of the night. It was a relief to know they also had body clocks. Perhaps that's the answer for tourists visiting Lapland in summer: become nocturnal, as it seems the Sami are.

THIRTEEN

From Lapland to Scotland

Part of the reason for our visit to Lapland in June 2003 was to investigate the possibility of importing more reindeer from Sweden to improve the genetics of our own herd in Scotland. Anyone who breeds animals will tell you that it is important to avoid inbreeding, and with a closed herd like ours bringing in new blood can only be an advantage. The last introduction of new blood was in 1995, when we were gifted a captive herd of reindeer from the Jura Mountains in France. Our time with Jussa in Vaisaluokta had been the most fruitful of our trips to Lapland to investigate sources of reindeer to strengthen our herd, and having spent the summer negotiating we struck a deal to buy reindeer from his herd. Jussa would look after them in quarantine, and then we would transport them back to Scotland to join up with our reindeer there. The reindeer would be chosen during the time of the bull slaughter in the autumn.

September saw Alan and I back in arctic Sweden to choose our reindeer. Autumn in the Arctic is the most colourful time of year, with all the deciduous trees and shrubs turning colour. Everywhere we looked there were reds and yellows, oranges and browns, and, like the vegetation, the reindeer too were changing colour as their new winter coats grew in. Frosty nights and bright days with the odd flurry of snow told us winter was not far round the corner. Our first task was to find a vet to monitor the quarantine, perform all the necessary tests and fill in all the paperwork to satisfy British importation regulations. Our search took us to the town of Gallivare, where we met up with Peter Zaff, a Swedish state veterinarian, in premises reminiscent of Reindeer House.

There was no doubt some order amid the chaos, and it turned out that he was in the process of moving premises. Peter was fantastically enthusiastic and agreed to perform all the necessary tests. He spoke impeccable English, and it turned out that he had been seconded to Britain to assist in the foot and mouth crisis in 2001.

Choosing our Reindeer

Alan and I went to join Jussa and his brother, Per Ola, at one of the reindeer bull slaughter sites up in the mountains. Less remote than the one at Vaisaluotka, these corrals could almost be reached by car along forestry tracks, leaving about an hour's walk up into the hills. We left the car with about twenty others and joined the steady stream of people walking up through the forest on to the open hill. There were a few people on quad bikes and motorbikes, some towing trailers. It was definitely a day out for the whole family. It transpired that it was also a field trip for the local school.

As with the calf marking in June, a herd of reindeer had been gathered into a corral. This time, though, there were about 5,000 reindeer in an area the size of a football stadium. It was a spectacular sight with bulls in full antler, the velvet stripped from them ready for the rut, and the cows and the calves just beginning to lose the velvet off their antlers. After a summer of browsing on the mountain vegetation the reindeer were all in the peak of condition. With their fat reserves to see them through the lean winter ahead, it was the perfect time to slaughter the animals for meat. As the herd moved around the large corral, people stood ready with their lassoos. The first job was to mark any calves that had slipped through the net at calf marking in the summer. In the same way as before, the calves had to be identified from their mothers' ear marks. The vast majority of calves had been marked earlier in the year and the stragglers were soon picked off. Then small groups of reindeer were driven into a smaller corral where individual bulls were lassoed and dragged through a gate into a long corridor. These were the ones chosen for slaughter. The bulls destined for meat varied in age from 18 months to perhaps 5 years. It was a physically

Autumn corral of reindeer to select bulls for slaughter.

demanding process, with uncooperative bulls leaping around on the end of a rope. The corridor that the bulls were put into was a mile long and 200yds wide. At the end of the day the whole group was pushed down the corridor to holding pens, where the slaughtering would take place the next day.

It was at this stage that we were allowed to choose our reindeer. Our main criteria was tameness. The young bulls that kicked up a fuss, lashing out with their hooves and giving the handlers grief, we avoided; the quieter, more genteel ones we chose.

Harvesting the reindeer for meat is the main source of revenue for the Sami, and the by-products of the process, skins and antlers, are mainly used in the Sami craft industry. Reindeer meat is widely available in the north of Sweden in fresh, smoked and dried form, and is the staple diet for Sami families. Compared with farmed animals such as cattle or

Skinning reindeer. It was reassuring to observe that every bit of the carcass was utilised.

sheep, there is no contest when it comes to good husbandry and welfare. These reindeer have spent their entire lives in their natural environment with no artificial feeding, drugs or growth hormones. If it weren't all consumed in Sweden, reindeer meat would be a perfect alternative to organic meat in Britain today.

Kuorpaks Sameviste, the bull slaughter site, was thronged with people the next day. By the time we arrived many reindeer had already been killed (using a humane killer), bled, skinned and hung up. Having picked out our reindeer from the group, we set to work helping with the skinning, gutting and cleaning. Every last bit of a reindeer carcass is utilised: the blood, whipped to prevent it curdling, is made into blood pudding; the intestines, cleaned, are used for sausages skins; and even the leg skins are cured to make footwear. Most prized was the net of fat and thin connective tissue found around the stomach. Carefully removed, this would be used to fry with. There was no waste, which was good to see, bearing in mind we live in such a wasteful society today.

As the day drew to a close all the bulls in the pens were dealt with, but it became apparent that there were more reindeer on the way. What we couldn't imagine was just how these reindeer would actually arrive. Suddenly there was frantic activity as cars pulling flat trailers drove to a clearing in the forest in response to the hum of a distant helicopter. As it came closer we could make out a bundle of dead reindeer dangling below it; the pilot carefully lowered his cargo on to the waiting trailers and then buzzed away for another load. These reindeer had been dispatched at a more remote slaughter site and now needed to be skinned and gutted too. In Swedish Lapland today there are estimated to be 280,000 domesticated reindeer, and on average 20 per cent of the population is slaughtered for meat each year in the autumn and winter. It is a busy time for the Sami.

Quarantine, Training and Transporting Home

From Kuorpaks Sameviste we transported our group of reindeer to enclosures close to Jussa's home. They would stay here in quarantine for the next four months, after which we would return to take them home to Scotland. The quarantine regulations for reindeer, like all cloven-hoofed animals, require a test for tuberculosis, which has to be done at the beginning of the quarantine period and then again four months later at the end of the period. Indeed, it is the tuberculosis test that sets the parameters of four months' isolation. But, as Peter Zaff pointed out, Sweden was free of bovine tuberculosis and had been for many years – so he was testing for a disease that did not actually exist in Sweden! Nevertheless, rules are rules. With our small band of reindeer left in the more than capable hands of Jussa and Per Ola, we headed for home. Christmas, our busy time, was looming and soon we would be out and about with our teams of trained reindeer, opening Santa's Grotto, switching on Christmas lights and taking part in Christmas parades. It all seemed a far cry from the harvesting of reindeer meat in Swedish Lapland.

Our return to arctic Sweden at the beginning of February made us appreciate just what rigorous conditions reindeer have to endure during the winter months. Our main aim, before transporting our reindeer home, was to handle them as much as we could, haltering them, leading them around and tethering them up, so that they would be accustomed to us handling them on the five-day journey home. This was all done in average temperatures each day of −20 °C, although on the coldest day the thermometer dropped to −35 °C. The snow lay deep on the ground and hung heavy on the trees. Although we had come well prepared with extra pairs of thick socks, padded clothes and down-filled jackets, the cold was intense. Any warm air we breathed out immediately froze on our chins and our feet weren't just cold, they felt like blocks of ice. Unlike the reindeer, we could of course retreat to the warmth of the locals' houses, with their triple glazing and central heating. When I mentioned to Jussa how cold my feet were while we were working with the reindeer, he produced a pair of reindeer skin boots which he had bought from a Russian Sami and insisted that the next day I wear them to keep my feet warm. They were made entirely of reindeer skin, double layered so there was reindeer hair on the inside and the outside, but there was no sole which meant that I felt as though I was walking around in my slippers! Yet the difference was amazing: my feet remained cosy and warm in these boots. The only problem was that they had no grip, so I was regularly to be seen skiing along behind runaway reindeer.

Training reindeer Sami style was rather different from our own methods. They invariably used a lasso to catch them, so as soon as a lasso appeared the reindeer were away in the opposite direction. We needed to gain their confidence and encourage them to approach us. When we appeared without the lasso, a few of the tamer animals approached us. In a small corral we were able to halter them by enticing them with lichen, and then we walked them around and tethered them up, rewarding their good behaviour with titbits. With the tamest ones out of the way, the next tamest ones came forward looking for food, and in the same way were haltered, led around and tethered. By the time we came to the wildest ones, though, the lasso was needed. Every day we repeated the procedure, starting at first light, slowly getting to know the reindeer and of course letting them get to know us. Every so often someone would wander out of their cosy houses to

Halter training in Sweden. All the reindeer we chose to take back to Scotland needed some handling before we left – some were more reluctant than others.

watch us at work. The Sami were intrigued by our different approach and impressed by our dogged determination to train each reindeer to be led quietly on a halter. We were encouraged to stop every couple of hours to go inside and eat. I don't think I had ever eaten so much so often. But, as they explained, in such cold conditions you have to keep your calorie intake up. As we got to know them, we gave each reindeer a Sami name, such as Rákkas, Mosski, Ritsem, Sarek, Sirkas and Ola. After a week our small herd of nineteen reindeer were as ready as they would ever be for the journey ahead. Peter Zaff came to do the final health check on the group; deeming them fit to travel, and with the copious paperwork in order, we were on our way at last.

For three days we travelled by livestock truck, with three overnight stops on the way. Our destination was the port of Hantsholm in north Denmark, to embark on a ferry that would take us across the North Sea to Shetland. Our lorry driver was particularly looking forward to the trip, because he was planning to fill up his truck with cheap Danish alcohol before returning to Sweden, where alcohol is extortionately expensive. The three days spent on the lorry went very smoothly. Indeed, it was quite likely that the reindeer were used to travelling in lorries, because in modern-day Lapland many of the reindeer are transported in this way between summer and winter grazing. At Hantsholm we off-loaded the reindeer into special livestock containers, the type they use for transporting sheep and cattle from the Shetlands to the mainland. These containers are open at the top and gated all the way round, with internal partitions that allowed us to split the reindeer into small groups. Each group was bedded down on straw, with food and water within easy reach. Then we waited on the dockside, along with the passengers for the trip back to the Faroe Isles via Shetland. The ferry is the main form of communication for the Faroese, delivering inhabitants, tourists and everyday food and commodities from Denmark.

The reindeer were the last to be loaded, which pleased us as it meant they would be the first to disembark. Placed in

Our Swedish reindeer crossing the North Sea en route to the Cairngorms. The open-topped livestock containers were ideal for transporting the reindeer and when bedded with straw and well ventilated, it meant our animals could be fed and watered easily during the journey.

the main hull of the boat, we would have to endure the roar of the engines for the 20-hour crossing. Luckily the weather was fine, and the sea offered no more than a gentle swell. The reindeer seemed quite relaxed in their unusual surroundings and eagerly ate their food.

Coming Home

At last we saw land as we approached Lerwick in Shetland. So far, so good. We had reached the final stages of the journey with no mishaps. But as we walked off the ferry behind the crates of reindeer, two very official-looking people approached us. Anxiously clutching the paperwork, I offered it to them as proof that the reindeer were *bona fide* and we had all the official stamps. But happily, that wasn't what they wanted to see at all, it was only our passports they were interested in. Lerwick harbour buzzed with media interest and journalists from the local radio and television stations were there to see reindeer in Shetland for the first time.

Although we still faced a 12-hour ferry journey to reach mainland Scotland, we were beaming from ear to ear. Our new reindeer had made it this far, and we felt we were on the home straight. Despite the stresses of the journey, our new Swedish reindeer were quite unfazed by the whole ordeal and when we reached home and joined them up with a few of our own reindeer, the Swedish boys won every tussle hands down. It was only a matter of time before they were fully integrated into our herd. The most bizarre thing about the whole trip was that at no point in Sweden, Denmark or Scotland did anyone ask to see the reindeer or indeed check the paperwork that went with them.

Mr Utsi had always been very careful to ensure that the reindeer he brought in came from a number of different genetic strains. And over the years solitary bulls had been introduced to improve the bloodlines. This import of new blood would keep the genetics of our Scottish reindeer sound for a long time to come, with the added bonus that the whole project gave us a tremendous insight into life with reindeer in Lapland today.

FOURTEEN

Scottish Reindeer Tales

Over a dram one day with our neighbour, farmer Jimmy MacArthur, I was describing the problems we sometimes faced with our reindeer, in particular the rather unsavoury topic of death. Reindeer, I explained, do have a bad habit of sometimes dropping dead for no apparent reason, even when they appear to be in the finest condition. Jimmy had farmed all his life and had a philosophical answer to my frustrations. 'When you have livestock,' he said, 'you have dead stock,' knocking back his whisky in one gulp. This is some comfort when you've tried your best and the worst happens.

Reindeer are most difficult to rear in captivity. Their dietary requirements are quite specific and, unless you can recreate arctic tundra in the summer and lichen heaths in the winter, there will inevitably be health problems. This is why reindeer are not particularly popular animals to have on display in zoos, and why they never became a farmed animal kept in fields like cows and sheep. They need to live as natural a life as possible. Our Scottish reindeer are a compromise: they are free ranging on natural vegetation for part of the year but when it becomes necessary they are brought in and fed. It is a balancing act that we have refined through years of hands-on experience.

Drop Dead Fred

One of the trickiest things to do is hand-rear a young, motherless calf. Apart from the obvious problems of finding a substitute for the rich reindeer milk, the orphaned calf tends to become a bit of a misfit, often being shunned by the rest of the herd, and generally regarding itself as partly human. Jura, Beauty, Dubh and Utsi are all successfully hand-reared reindeer. They probably survived because their mothers were able to raise them for at least the first week. Reindeer colostrum and the first few days of rich milk provide a great boost for any reindeer calf.

So it was a bold step for us to take a new-born calf away from his mother when he was just hours old. Marie, the mother, was notorious for losing her calves when they were just a few days old. We suspected she didn't produce enough milk. This had happened once too often, so we decided to 'bite the bullet' and try to raise her next calf ourselves. Taking her calf away was traumatic for Marie. Reindeer are good mothers, and for days afterwards she would challenge us on the hill, as if to say 'what have you done with my calf?' It was up to us to prove to her that we had done the right thing. We rather perversely decided to call the baby Fred, after the rather comical film *Drop Dead Fred*.

Goat's milk is the best substitute for reindeer milk, and every two hours, night and day, Fred drank his milk. He never looked back, progressing to fewer bottles of milk supplemented with lichens and leaves. He lived in an outside pen beside the back door. (Even calves will overheat if you bring them inside.) Our daily routine all that summer was regulated by Fred's feeding times. By the time he was a month old we thought it was time for us to have a break, so we left him for the afternoon and went off to the local Highland Games at Newtonmore.

Unfortunately, Fred's first afternoon alone could not have been worse. While we were away there was an almighty thunderstorm with torrential rain. When we returned from our afternoon out Fred was drenched and exhausted; he had only enough energy to stumble through the door into the house and collapse on the floor in a heap. That night we resigned ourselves to the fact that Fred was going to die. Reindeer are not great fighters, and when the chips are down they are quite happy to turn up their toes and give in. As the evening wore on there was very little change. However, at about 10 p.m. Fred uttered a grunt, indicating that he was

Drop Dead Fred. In 2001 Fred made the front cover and was the centre-fold picture in the Saturday edition of the *Daily Telegraph* colour supplement (22 December 2001).

hungry. We couldn't believe it: perhaps Fred *was* going to survive. With some warm milk inside him, life seemed to return to his limp, cold body. It seemed that Fred wasn't going to give up that easily.

Happily Fred recovered completely from his drenching but soon he had to face another threat to his life. It transpired he was born with a hernia. If the vet didn't operate on it while he was still young, it could well lead to serious complications when he was older. Having invested a great deal of time and emotion into this young reindeer, it seemed only sensible to give him the best chance for the future, so we agreed to the operation. General anaesthetic for reindeer is not exactly a common request, and on the few occasions it has been used there was great concern as to the amount needed. Too much, and they'll never wake up. The operation was performed on the kitchen table at Reindeer House, because 2001 was the year of the Foot and Mouth outbreak and there was a ban on moving cloven-hoofed animals in a bid to stop the disease spreading. Leaving our two vets, Andrew and Jane, in charge, I decided to take a walk. I couldn't bear to watch, and there was nothing I could do after we had manhandled an unconscious Fred up on to the makeshift operating table. When I returned the job was done, and Fred lay flat out on the floor in the sitting room. Now we just had to wait for him to wake up.

A few hours seemed to go by. We had to step over Fred's prostrate body on the floor, while the dogs circumnavigated him. He continued to breathe and his eyelids twitched, but nothing more than that. Eventually, to try to jolt him back to consciousness, we decided to offer him a bottle of his favourite goat's milk. To our delight his nose twitched and with some difficulty he raised his head to reach for the teat. Hunger had got the better of him, and it would just be a question of time now before he was back on his feet again. Despite a couple of close calls, Drop Dead Fred has survived to tell his tale. Perhaps there is something in a name!

Burgundy and Shock

Burgundy was almost perfect. She was one of the best-looking reindeer in the herd; she always grew spectacular antlers and invariably was in fine condition. She was a perfect reindeer to have in the herd really – except that she had never produced a calf. This frustrated us as we wanted her to pass her good looks on to the next generation. It evidently frustrated her, too. Every year during the calving season she would look longingly at the other cows with their calves, and pestered her mother Tuna incessantly, even muscling in when she gave birth and trying to steal the young calf away from her. You could guarantee that the day Tuna headed off to find a quiet place to calve Burgundy would be hot on her heels. And a few days later the trio would turn up again, Burgundy looking as pleased as Punch and Tuna resigned to the fact that she would have to share her calf for another year. This went on for a number of years until at last, at the age of 9, we suspected that Burgundy herself was in calf. As the winter came to a close she certainly seemed to expand round her

Burgundy and Shock. Some things are worth waiting for – even nine years!
Shock has matured into one of our finest male reindeer.

girth, but the most telling sign was a developing udder. Our suspicions were confirmed in May 2000 when Burgundy headed off to calve. Following a long, protracted calving, and with the help of our vet, out popped a great big bull calf which we promptly named Shock – a state of mind that Burgundy was definitely in! Delighted with the new arrival, she enthusiastically licked the little chap bone dry. Shock had all his mum's good looks and has matured into one of our finest males. Despite calving for the first time late in life, Burgundy went on to have a succession of calves.

She's Mine!

The calving season is always a time to look forward to. It's the only way we can regularly increase our reindeer numbers and young calves are some of the most delightful creatures you could wish to meet. But sometimes the delight of these enchanting animals is marred by tragedy. In the spring of 2002 Sleet, a mature white female, calved first. A strapping female calf was born and the pair of them seemed to be very healthy. Sleet obviously had plenty of milk because the calf was very strong and growing well. But then disaster struck. While out checking on the cows with their new arrivals, I noticed that Sleet and her calf were missing. I went to look for them and came upon one of the most pitiful scenes I have ever faced in all my time with the herd. Sleet was lying dead and her calf was crawling over her, I suppose in an effort to 'wake her up'. Sleet must have died very suddenly, perhaps of milk fever, because there was no sign that she was ailing. Our only choice was to take the calf off the hill and hand-rear her. For a couple of days we kept her at Reindeer House and tried to get her to take milk from a bottle. This is never an easy task when the calf is used to tasty reindeer milk from a warm udder. Just as we were getting somewhere, another cow, Herald, calved a stillborn calf. We decided to try to pair her up with the orphaned calf. Just as shepherds skin dead lambs and drape the skin over orphan lambs to kid the ewe into taking the stranger, so we tried the same trick with the orphan calf. But there were a few problems. First, Sleet's calf was white and the dead calf was black, so it was inevitable that Herald would notice the difference. Also, the orphan was beginning to get used to us and wasn't so sure she wanted a reindeer mother after all. But we persevered and shut the pair away in a pen on their own. Every few hours we held Herald and encouraged the calf to suckle. Soon the little calf began to look forward to the milk bar. Herald was reluctant at first, to say the least, but as the days went by the calf seemed to grow on her and she even began to grunt to the calf. Before long the two were firmly bonded to each other, and we let them back into the main herd. The naming theme that year was 'Gold' because it was the fiftieth year of reindeer in Scotland – our golden anniversary, if you like. So when it came to naming Sleet's calf we chose Mine (as in Gold Mine!) because no doubt that's what Herald ended up saying when she finally accepted her new calf.

Reign of Terror

You would be forgiven for thinking that this heading was hatched up by a tabloid newspaper. Sadly it was, and embarrassingly it refers to one of our own Cairngorm reindeer. The combination of rampant hormones and hill walkers being in the wrong place at the wrong time led to an extremely unfortunate sequence of events, which we hope will never be repeated.

It was autumn, the height of the rutting season for reindeer, and the testosterone levels in the herd were at their peak. We had two breeding groups, one kept in our large hill enclosure, and the other free ranging on the Cairngorm Mountains. Utsi was strutting his stuff with his harem of females in the enclosure while his sparring partner Cluster was out on the free range with another group of cows. There was nothing unusual about this: we always liked to run a couple of breeding groups to make the most of the breeding potential.

It was a late Sunday afternoon, and it had been a fine day on the hill, perfect for walkers. Unfortunately, it was also a fine day for Cluster to flex his muscles and show off in front of his girls. A man and his wife came into the Reindeer Centre in an extremely agitated state. It transpired that they had just encountered a reindeer bull on the mountainside, and he was less than friendly. Indeed, it turned out that Cluster, probably feeling intimidated by their nearness to his females, decided to have a go at the gentleman with his antlers, ripping his rather expensive jacket and obviously frightening him. The man's wife, in an attempt to stop the attack, had the presence of mind to throw hot tea from her thermos on to Cluster's head, which luckily stopped him in his tracks and gave the couple a chance to get away. They then hurried down to the Reindeer Centre to report the incident. It had happened on the hill at about 3,500ft, close to a well-walked path. There was no vehicular access on to the hill, so one of our colleagues, Morna, had to walk up as quickly as she could to locate Cluster and prevent him assaulting any more unsuspecting walkers. As she headed up the ridge she was alarmed to see a mountain rescue helicopter leaving the hillside, not far from where she expected to find Cluster with his cows. She was even more worried when she caught up with Cluster and found the front blade of his antler was covered in blood. What the hell had he done? Morna stayed with the group of reindeer till nightfall to warn off any passers-by, and then at first light a posse of reindeer herders and the local vet with his tranquilliser gun headed up the hill to subdue Cluster, cut off his antlers and lead him down off the hill. In the meantime the telephone never stopped ringing: the whole world wanted to get the story of the raging bull reindeer.

Cluster, now antlerless and enclosed, posed no more threat to walkers in the hills but the rest of the gory story had yet to be heard. It turned out that soon after the first couple had fled the scene, two men walked over the brow of the hill and were confronted by Cluster, already wound up from his previous altercation. His reaction was to dig his antler into one man's leg before gathering his females and heading off. This explained the blood that Morna saw on his antlers. Luckily the men had a mobile phone, and managed to get help by phoning mountain rescue. The rescue helicopter took the injured man to hospital, where the wound was sufficient to need stitches. Various stories about the attacks were told in the tabloid newspapers – stories that greeted Alan and I on our return from our first holiday for nine years! That the owners 'declined to comment about the incident' was well wide of the truth. The fact was we were halfway up Mount Kilimanjaro at the time and knew nothing about it. Cluster had definitely 'cooked his goose' as a rutting bull. The following summer he was the first to be castrated.

Homeward Bound

We tend to take for granted the feats of navigation animals are able to perform without previous experience or technical equipment to help them. Hump-backed whales, arctic terns and Barren Ground Caribou all migrate vast distances by means of a sort of innate GPS, so it should come as no surprise that our reindeer can get themselves from A to B with no previous knowledge of the terrain they are crossing. Our reindeer normally confine their wanderings to the mountain environment they know, and they have a strong homing instinct that brings them back to their home ground, the northern slopes of the Cairngorms, at some point in the year. Unless something untoward has happened, reindeer who have gone walkabout tend to turn up eventually during the rut looking for the opposite sex.

But one of our reindeer, Lilac, went one stage further in her bid to get home. Since 1990 the Cairngorm reindeer have been split into two herds, one remaining on the original site on the Cairngorms and the second based about 30 miles away on the Glenlivet Estate near Tomintoul. Lilac had spent all her young life on the Cairngorms but was moved by livestock trailer with a number of other reindeer to Glenlivet during the winter of 2004 when she was 6 years old.

The winter grazing for our reindeer at Glenlivet is an isolated range of hills to the north of the Cairngorm Mountains, surrounded by hill farms, grouse moors, roads and rivers. Although the reindeer can see the Cairngorms from here, they have never been tempted to try to get there, seeming quite happy in their new home. But that was not the case with Lilac. Within a couple of weeks of arrival at the Glenlivet herd, she disappeared, taking with her another younger reindeer called Bell. We soon caught up with Bell, who had been thwarted by a fence and a road, and assumed from her location that Lilac was heading in the general direction of the Cairngorms. Lilac was obviously a more determined reindeer because two weeks later she turned up with the Cairngorm herd at feed time. On her travels she would have encountered a number of physical obstacles, including numerous stock fences, roads, rivers and unknown hill ground. But her homing instinct was strong, and on the basis of her achievement we didn't have the heart to take her back to Glenlivet. In any case she would probably have just found her own way back again.

Dog's Dinner

Reindeer and dogs are not a good combination, bearing in mind the fact that wolves are the main predator of reindeer. And it is distressing for us that a number of reindeer deaths, particularly of calves in the summer months in the Cairngorms, are due to dog worrying. These are not wild dogs roaming loose and ownerless in the mountains. These are people's pets, who are out in the hills with their owners. Tragically for our reindeer, they are out of control. In the early days dog worrying gave Mr Utsi a lot of grief and he was constantly on the lookout for walkers whose dogs were out of control. Of course in those early days any disturbance or death among a small group of vulnerable reindeer still finding their feet in Scotland would have been a big loss. Sadly, fifty years on and more and there is still a percentage of the population who are happy to let their dogs roam over sensitive areas like the Cairngorm Mountains, causing havoc, not just among our resident population of reindeer but also among vulnerable ground-nesting birds.

In the twenty-five years I have been with the reindeer I think the worst incident of dog worrying took place in the autumn of 1998, when a four-month-old reindeer calf called Aero was attacked by two collie dogs. It was a Sunday afternoon and it had been a glorious day on the hill after a frosty start. Days like this always bring out the hill walkers, and this day was no exception. At about 5 p.m. the phone rang. It was a man who had just witnessed the reindeer herd being chased by two collie dogs. The dogs had then split off a calf from the herd and chased it into the burn, where they managed to get hold of it. He watched as the owner of the dogs eventually retrieved his dogs, put them in his car and drove away. Incensed by the owner's callous reaction, the man rang us at Reindeer House to explain what had happened. He described the calf as lying in the burn badly injured but still alive. The rest of the reindeer were, not surprisingly, nowhere to be seen. When I got up to the scene of the attack, with our 13-year-old son Alex, I was amazed to see the calf clamber to his feet and walk out of the burn despite his wounds. We managed to herd him the mile or so down to our enclosures, where we would be able to catch him in the smaller pens. Luckily the incident had also been witnessed by somebody who had the foresight to ring the local vet, and so by the time Aero reached the enclosure our vet Jane had arrived to treat his wounds. His injuries were sickening. The skin had been ripped off his hindquarters on both sides and his tail and rectum had been bitten off. Jane was able to put her hand right up the calf's back under the skin. He had basically been skinned alive. Luckily the injuries were fresh, so Jane immediately set to work stitching the patchwork of skin back together and cleaning the affected areas. We felt sure that the trauma of the incident and the extent of the injuries would prove too much for the calf and he would be dead by morning. Indeed, that might have been the best outcome for the calf, who had without doubt suffered enough.

I am not sentimental about reindeer. They are mortal like us, and they have to die sometime, but I was particularly angry about this incident. How could a dog owner distance himself from such a dreaful attack, and worse still, how could he just leave a calf that was so badly mauled. As I went up the hill the next morning I was convinced the calf would be dead, so I was shocked to find him walking about. Indeed the sight reduced me to tears because I knew that it would be a long haul bringing this courageous young reindeer back to full fitness. Armed with the owner's car registration number, I went to our local police station to report the incident. I was dismayed to find that reindeer are not classified as domesticated animals in Scottish law, so the police could do nothing.

I turned to the Scottish Society for the Prevention of Cruelty to Animals. I felt sure that the extent of Aero's injuries would persuade them to take the matter forward. However, their officer's reaction was equally disappointing. They would take no further action. Finally I tried to persuade the local paper to highlight our predicament with dogs. The editor was sympathetic and shocked by the extent of Aero's injuries, and agreed to make the lead story, but unfortunately he refused to publish the graphic photograph that would have brought home to readers the danger that unruly pets pose to our herd. He felt it would be too distressing for the readers. Despite his awful injuries, Aero survived and matured into a fine young reindeer, although he remained minus a tail. Luckily the vast majority of owners have control of their dogs and severe injuries like this are thankfully rare.

Glenlivet Exiles

One of the great advantages to our second reindeer site at Glenlivet is that reindeer blessed with a mischievous nature can be moved over there, keeping them out of the way of people either walking in the hills or joining us on our daily visits to the herd. Quite often naughty reindeer are ones that have been hand-reared like Utsi or Fred, but Monsoon is just naturally mischievous. Indeed, he comes from a long line of badly behaved reindeer. His grandfather Ole had a bad habit of lifting ladies' skirts with his antlers during hill visits and Lappi his mother was in the habit of smacking people with her front feet when she wasn't getting enough food.

Monsoon is a big strong reindeer, very bold and greedy, who stands no nonsense from any one. He is not frightened of dogs and is a nuisance when we are trying to move the herd using our own collie, because he will challenge her and smack her with his front feet if she gets too close. He was sent into exile at Glenlivet after an incident that occurred in late winter when he was out on the free range with the rest of the herd. An unsuspecting lady was out on the hills walking her small terrier, a Scotty dog. Monsoon spotted them and headed over to make sure the dog knew who was boss. Alarmed, the lady took flight, scooping the dog up and running down the hill with Monsoon in hot pursuit. Fortunately for her, she took the path alongside our reindeer enclosures and one of our people saw what was happening. Monsoon was soon diverted from his bullying behaviour by the offer of food, much to the relief of the lady. Monsoon lives at Glenlivet all the time now.

Fred has a similar disregard for dogs but his real failing is that he is too humanised, and an amorous reindeer is not necessarily everybody's cup of tea. He was always very popular on the hill visits because he stayed with us all the time, probably feeling more at home with human company and enjoying all the attention and extra food. As his greed increased, so his tactics became ever more outrageous. On one celebrated occasion, though, Fred overstepped the mark. Everyone on the visit was enjoying hand-feeding the reindeer and the reindeer were clamouring to get an extra handful. In his eagerness to get to the food Fred jumped up and knocked over a young lad, who landed face down in the wet boggy ground. As the boy's father leaned over to retrieve his son, Fred promptly knocked him face down in the mud too. It was quite funny really, although I'm not sure the father and son would agree. Fred had gone too far this time, so he too ended up living permanently at Glenlivet.

Utsi was also exiled as a result of his playful antics. I had received a few reports of a reindeer out on the Cairngorms who wasn't being aggressive towards people but seemed to be playing with them. He was a young bull with an impressive set of antlers, and the uninitiated were probably worried by his advances. One day I was heading out along the northern corries path with a bag of feed and a small group of vistors keen to see the herd. Suddenly, around the corner came a lady and her child, scurrying along hand in hand, with Utsi in hot pursuit, dancing, kicking his heels and tossing his head. He was not connecting with his victims but was just full of high jinks and enjoying the reaction he was getting. Of course as soon as he saw me, and more particularly the bag of feed on my back, he turned into a normal well-behaved reindeer. Meekly he turned tail and followed us out to where we met the rest of the herd. I had caught him red-handed, and Utsi's fate was sealed. Along with Fred and Monsoon, he is now a permanent resident at Glenlivet. So be warned if you encounter the Glenlivet herd on the hills while out walking – you can expect a few misfits to give you a hard time.

FIFTEEN

The Story of Christmas

For Christians around the world Christmas is the principal religious festival, but in fact it derived from an ancient pagan festival, Yuletide, which was celebrated on 21 December, the shortest day of the year. For our forebears living at higher latitudes, this was an extremely important time of the year. If the harvest had been good and there was sufficient stored food to get to this stage, then it deserved a celebration. From then on the days would get longer and they could look forward to better weather and the new growing season.

Pagan Vikings also celebrated the turn of the year, dressing up as Old Man Winter and making him as welcome as possible. The British eventually adopted the habit, and Old Man Winter became Father Christmas after the advent of Christianity. Still he was offered food and mead to keep him happy in the hope that his benevolence would ensure a mild winter and fruitful spring. Santa Claus came from over the Atlantic Ocean with his eight reindeer, and went on widely to be accepted as the giver of presents. Over time, these two characters, Father Christmas and Santa Claus, by now far removed from St Nicholas, became interchangeable characters.

Mention reindeer to most people and they invariably think of Christmas, particularly the Western world, where as everybody knows on Christmas Eve Santa Claus visits each child's house on a sleigh pulled by flying reindeer. He seems to know which children have been good and deserve presents. His traditional method of access to a house was down the chimney, but it would seem that these days his magical powers allow him to enter regardless of whether there is a chimney or not. Each stocking or pillow case duly filled, Santa heads off, presumably at great speed to ensure he visits every child that night.

Flying Reindeer

Reindeer must be able to fly, otherwise Santa would never get round all the children to deliver their presents on Christmas Eve. But where did the idea of flying reindeer originate? Throughout northern cultures the use of fly agaric or fly amanta, the red and white toadstool with hallucinogenic properties, is well documented. These toadstools contain both ibotenic acid and muscimol. The latter has hallucinogenic properties, but when the mushroom is dried the ibotenic acid also turns into muscimol, making the mushroom many times more potent. Soviet mycologist B.V. Vasil'kov reported: 'It has long been noted that the intoxicated among primitive people are perceived as prophets, and that every kind of prophet and shaman for putting themselves in a state of "professional" intoxication and artificial psychosis used poisonous mushrooms.' And in Viking culture it has been suggested that the berserker knights ate mushrooms from the genus Amanita before throwing themselves bare-chested and madly into battle.

Shaman were known to use this mushroom to assist them in their flights to the spirit world, and this practice was widespread. Interestingly, the urine passed by the hallucinating shaman also had the same properties but in a less potent form. It is well documented that reindeer are very partial to human urine, particularly during the winter months. An early twentieth-century anthropologist, Harald Sverdrup, wrote: 'The night-vessel, a large wooden bowl, stands outside the tent beside a huge block of snow. It is emptied into this snow block, which in the morning is chopped up and given to the reindeer as a treat. To the reindeer the salt content is invaluable and the Chukchi leave nothing to waste.' So in actively seeking human urine which is sometimes 'drugged', the reindeer may hallucinate and fly. In the folk tales of the reindeer peoples reindeer are often perceived to fly, and on

Flying 'deer' depicted on standing stones at a Bronze Age burial site in northern Mongolia. It seems that 'flying' reindeer have been around for a long time.

the Bronze Age Mongolian deer stones 'deer' are depicted as flying. The reindeer-herding Nenet regard the shaman's drum as a sacred reindeer that transports him to the spirits.

Reindeer are very partial to mushrooms and in the late summer, before the first frost of winter, they provide a particularly rich source of food. Fly agaric is found throughout the boreal forest. We had a reindeer called Frostie in our Cairngorm herd, who, regular as clockwork, in late summer would appear to be intoxicated. The first time we put it down to his quirky character, but walking sideways and falling over was a bit over the top, even for the quirkiest reindeer! When he did the same thing the following year, we started to wonder if he was eating some hallucinatory mushrooms. Certainly in our birch woodlands we have fly agaric. Perhaps Frostie was one of Santa Claus's reindeer. But his habit cost him his life. Although he was mature when he died, I think his penchant for these mushrooms damaged his system and he didn't live to a grand old age.

Regarding Rudolph's Sex

In the run-up to Christmas most years I get a phone call from the media wanting to know what sex Rudolph is. Obviously his name would suggest that he is male but the smart people who have done their research know that the male reindeer lose their antlers at the end of the rutting season, long before Christmas. And of course Santa's reindeer must have antlers. So perhaps 'Rudolph' should actually be 'Ruby', since the female reindeer keep their antlers throughout the winter. Furthermore breeding bulls would be exhausted from the rut and in no condition to haul a heavy sleigh. Having said that, the females are not good candidates either because they are smaller than the males, less powerful and probably in calf. In addition, the females in general are feisty, highly strung and less trainable than the males.

Among reindeer peoples the pivotal reindeer is the castrated male. He not only acts as a decoy to lead the herd, but also pulls sledges, is packed with belongings and can be ridden. Rudolph, then, is obviously a castrate. Bull antlers are a secondary sexual characteristic linked to testosterone levels. Castration changes the hormone balance which inevitably affects the antler cycle, meaning that castrated reindeer often do not lose their antlers until after Christmas, sometimes keeping them until late in the winter. Another big advantage for Santa is that castrated bulls' antlers are less dense than those of the breeding bulls, and carrying a lighter load can only be an advantage when you have to do that much flying. It would seem that Rudolph is light-headed in more ways than one.

The Making of Santa Claus

St Nicholas, Old Man Winter and Father Christmas all generally dressed in drab-coloured clothes or animal furs.

Which one is Rudolph? The castrated male still in full velvet on the right is Rudolph.

During Victorian times in Britain Father Christmas's cloak was emerald green with white fur trim, so why is it that today Santa Claus is always dressed in red and white? There are various explanations. The Coca-Cola company naturally likes to claim credit since in 1931 they commissioned the young Swedish artist Haddon Sundbolm to redesign Santa Claus for their winter advertising campaign. Sundbolm drew him as a larger-than-life figure in a red cloak with white fur trim, held in place by a thick leather belt. His pipe was replaced by a bottle of coke. For the next fifty years this compelling image was seen around the world.

Although Coca-Cola would like to think they created today's Santa, in fact a number of other artists had already depicted him as rotund and jolly, and Louis Prang of the *Boston Press* dressed him in red and white garb for a Christmas card in 1885. However, the hugely influential Coca-Cola campaign definitely cemented his image forever.

Our Christmas Reindeer

The Cairngorm reindeer originally came from domesticated stock so their friendliness and trust towards humans has been ingrained into them over thousands of years – indeed in this respect they are no different from a horse or a dog. This is why we decided to borrow Santa's popularity and train our reindeer to pull sleighs at Christmas time. In the early days Mr Utsi delighted the local children with his reindeer at Christmas, but now we have several teams of reindeer that spend November and December taking part in street parades, switching on Christmas lights, making television advertisements and delivering Santa to his grotto all over Britain. The castrated male reindeer are big, strong and tractable, and completely unfazed by their stardom. And when Christmas Day arrives, they go back to the mountains for the next ten months. It's not a bad life really. And it is this long period of freedom that justifies what we do with them. Reindeer *need* the hills and mountains, the lichen heath in winter and the large open spaces to graze. Without them they are not truly reindeer.

Christmas in Aviemore, 1954. Niklaus Labba in full Sami dress with a reindeer and sleigh entertaining the local children.

Christmas today for the Cairngorm reindeer – sleigh-pullers Tiger and Iceberg ready for the off at the National Trust for Scotland's Crathes Castle, Royal Deeside, 2004.

As Christmas Eve is the only night of the year when reindeer fly, the rest of the time they have to travel more conventionally by lorry. Bedded with straw, they soon lie down and arrive at their destination ready for a bowl of food. Many a petrol station attendant has been astonished and thrilled to get a glimpse of the reindeer as we stop to fill up with fuel, and the reception we get at events from adults and children alike is invariably of joy and fascination. 'I've never seen a reindeer before' is a very common comment. I think if I was 5 years old and saw Santa with real reindeer, I would be hugely impressed. The question of which one is Rudolph always arises, but of course he can't do all the work so his friends have to help him out before the big night.

S I X T E E N

Rudolph's Future

With a current world population of approximately 6 million, reindeer and caribou as a species are not endangered. But their habitat is being constantly eroded away as a result of the exploitation of its valuable resources, ranging from the logging of timber in the great northern forests to the extraction of minerals, oil and gas from the tundra. In addition, the infrastructure associated with these industries directly affects the natural movements and grazing patterns of both domestic and wild herds of *Rangifer tarandus*. The roads that service the industries and the pipelines that carry oil are massive physical barriers impeding the daily movements of migrating herds. And on top of all this the climate seems to be changing.

Global Warming

There is no denying the physics of it. More greenhouse gases will mean more warming, and one of the areas of the world that is most susceptible to this is at the poles. Carbon dioxide, a natural and essential ingredient of all living systems, is a major player in this process. Carbon dioxide (and other gases with similar properties) in the atmosphere converts light into energy and traps it. Since most of the atmospheric carbon dioxide exists below the higher clouds, the light energy it converts to heat is temporarily trapped near the earth's surface.

Animals, engines driven by fossil fuels and volcanoes are all sources of greenhouse gases, and all are continually making deposits into the atmosphere. To counteract this process, oceans, coral reefs, forests of trees and the arctic tundra act as sinks, in effect drawing off carbon dioxide from the atmosphere. It is the apparent upsetting of the delicate balance between these two basic processes that is causing the concerns of today. And the problem lies largely in the huge increase of carbon dioxide being deposited in the atmosphere by man's activities, which far exceeds the ability of the counteracting processes to reabsorb the gases. Today nobody can realistically deny that global warming is an issue, but the debate revolves around the accuracy of various computer models predicting a range of future scenarios from 'nothing to worry about' to 'the end of the world as we know it'.

The Melting Arctic

For a number of decades the effects of global warming have been most apparent in the polar regions, where even a small increase in temperature can have dramatic results. The combination of rising surface air temperatures and warmer waters in the Arctic has led to a drastic decline in sea ice, particularly in the summer months. Sea ice is the main hunting ground for polar bears, and without it they will starve. How long before they become extinct?

Less obvious, but potentially just as serious in the future, is the potential loss of the far north as a net sink of carbon. The process of breaking down dead plant material, which results in the release of carbon, does not take place in wet boggy conditions because microbes which work on the dead plant material cannot work in wet anaerobic environments. Effectively carbon is taken out of the atmosphere in this way, locked up in the boggy environment of much of the tundra and taiga. However, in recent years it has been noticed that the far north is releasing more carbon than it is storing because many of the wet, boggy areas are drying up so helping to accelerate the greenhouse effect. There is also evidence of the permafrost melting in places and earlier, more vigorous plant growth. But a general trend in warming can be confused with natural variation and its knock-on effects, which may create warmer, wetter conditions in some areas and colder, drier conditions in others.

The problems of global warming in arctic and sub-arctic areas today are compounded by other factors and as a result the situation has become ever more challenging for reindeer, caribou and the northern people that live by these animals. The Sami in northern Europe are seeing their grazing pastures change as the weather becomes less predictable. People across the Arctic and Sub-arctic are reporting the spread of new species of animals, particularly insects. Coastlines are being battered and eroded by extreme weather conditions and vital routes, installations and pipelines are deteriorating because the permafrost is melting beneath them. All this is compounded by increasing industrial activity, its infrastructure and pollution, which directly affect populations of reindeer, caribou and the people that live by them.

Pipelines and Pollution

Pipelines and transport systems are known to affect where caribou calve. Studies of the Prudhoe Bay herd have shown that cows will avoid calving near pipelines and so their choice is restricted. For the cow and her vulnerable calf this can be critical, as their 'second choice' may have reduced food quality, thus jeopardising the calf's survival. During a spring of late snow melt females are forced to calve further away from the rich coastal plain and calf mortality is significantly increased.

In Russia heavy metals, radioactivity and sulphur dioxide pollution are all cited as threats to reindeer populations and the people that depend on them. Russia's track record during the Soviet years was appalling: in a bid to industrialise the far north huge tracts of land were decimated with a total disregard for the natural environment and the native people that lived there. Atmospheric nuclear explosions, commonplace in the Arctic from the end of the Second World War, released long-lasting radioactivity into the area. Compared with other northern mammals, reindeer and caribou were found to have particularly high radioactive contamination levels from this, due to their dependence on lichen as a source of food. Lichens absorb abnormally high

The unnatural side of the Arctic – oil pipelines at Prudhoe Bay, Alaska.

levels of radioactive fallout because of their ability to absorb nutrients directly from the air. This, combined with their very slow rate of growth, means they remain radioactive for a long time. The Chernobyl nuclear accident of 1986 reminded the world of the problems of radioactivity in reindeer and the cultures that depend on them.

Extensive logging of the boreal forest right across Eurasia and North America has also had a devastating effect on woodland populations of reindeer and caribou.

Rudolph in a Warmer World

Warmer summer conditions are likely to increase insect harassment for reindeer and caribou. This may have a knock-on effect on their body condition as they graze less and expend more energy in escaping from the biting insects. The arrival of new species of biting and sucking insects moving up from the south may impact on their health status too. An increase in rainfall could be critical for reindeer at certain times of year. Wet weather in the spring when the calves are born makes them particularly vulnerable and leads to higher mortality. Increased snow cover in the winter would mean the reindeer or caribou have to expend more energy digging and travelling to find food. In contrast, though, such conditions would permit an earlier spring flush of green plants that could benefit the cows with their young calves. It is a complicated picture, but it is likely that in the Arctic, where the ecosystems are relatively simple and closely interrelated, upsetting one will inevitably upset all the rest.

Unlike very specialised arctic animals like the polar bear, reindeer and caribou are mixed feeders and highly adaptive as a species. Their natural range covers a vast array of arctic and sub-arctic habitats. The Svalbard Reindeer and Peary Caribou of the high Arctic are sedentary and survive on a concoction of ground-hugging, high-arctic plants all year round. On the continental land masses of Siberia and North America similar animals make long seasonal migrations from the rich pastures of the mountain or coastal tundra in the summer to the nutrient-depleted lichen heaths of the boreal forests in the winter. Their diet is very different. Distinctive again is the diet of the reindeer introduced to South Georgia in the southern hemisphere, where the animals have come to rely almost exclusively on tussock grass. In general reindeer and caribou fared very well during the successive phases of natural warming that followed the series of Ice Ages, being able to adapt, migrate and re-establish themselves further north. Even though the Arctic and sub-Arctic are no longer the pristine wilderness of thousands of years ago, reindeer and caribou are great survivors. There is still hope for them.

Where to See Reindeer

The Cairngorm reindeer herd, Scotland

This offers the chance to join the reindeer herder out on the hillsides where the reindeer graze in their natural environment. These quiet, friendly animals are a delight to all ages. Each reindeer in the herd is an individual, with a name and a character all their own. If you approve of their lifestyle, why not support the herd by adopting one of them?

Visitors at the Cairngorm Reindeer Centre. It is very much a 'hands-on' experience and a unique opportunity to encounter reindeer in their natural environment.

During the months of November and December some of the big friendly male reindeer go out and about to various venues, as far south as Exeter and as far north as Thurso, delivering Father Christmas to his grotto. Keep your eyes open – they may come to your town. But don't worry, they will be back home in plenty of time for the big night – Christmas Eve!

Contact details:
The Cairngorm Reindeer Centre
Glenmore
Aviemore
Inverness-shire PH22 1QU
Tel/Fax: 01479 861228
www.reindeer-company.demon.co.uk
reindeerinfo@btinternet.com

Ajtte Swedish Mountain and Sami Museum, Jokkmokk, Swedish Lapland

Located in Jokkmokk on the Arctic Circle, the museum tells the story of Sapmi and the Sami people, of life and survival in a demanding climate and environment. Sapmi is the land of the Sami and extends without bounds across the territory of four nations, encompassing a vast area of mountainous and forested country, tundra and wetlands. Exhibits include stories of life from yesteryear to the present day; Laponia, Lapland's world heritage site; Sami costume; how people have adapted to life in a land without roads; and the migration of animals.

Contact details:
Ajtte Swedish Mountain and Sami Museum
Kyrkogatan 3
SE-962 23 Jokkmokk
Sweden
www.ajtte.com
info@ajtte.com

Jokkmokk Winter Market. The highlight of the market is the reindeer parade led by a Swedish Sami in full traditional dress.

Jokkmokk Winter Market

The winter market is held over four days beginning on the first Thursday in February. Sales of handicrafts and art, music concerts, lectures, reindeer and dog-sled races attract thousands of visitors from near and far. It is very cold at this time of year and several layers of clothing are the best way to stay warm. The highlight of each day is the reindeer parade, with pure white reindeer pulling traditional Lappish sleds. The first market was held in 1605, and has continued uninterrupted since then. It is a great opportunity to learn about the Sami's colourful culture.

Contact details:
Turism I Jokkmokk AB
Stortorget 4, Box 124
S-962 23 JOKKMOKK
Sweden
www.turism.jokkmokk.se

Sapmi Journeys

This company, based in the village of Jukkasjarvi, where the famous Icehotel is also to be found, specialises in the 'Sami Experience'. Tours include a reindeer safari, a cultural trip or a Lapland package tour with guides who have a direct connection with the Sami culture and their way of life.

Contact details:
Sapmi Journeys – Nutti Sami Siida AB
Marknadsvagen 11
981 91 Jukkasjarvi
Sweden
www.nutti.se
info@nutti.se

Rovaniemi, Finnish Lapland

If it's reindeer, snow and Santa Claus that you want, then this is the place to go. Rovaniemi, the capital of Finnish Lapland, is situated just inside the Arctic Circle. All year round you can visit the 'home of Santa', complete with village post office, toy factory and of course his house. Particularly during the run-up to Christmas, daily flights leave various destinations in Britain on package deals that include the return flight, a sleigh ride pulled by reindeer or dogs, a tour of Santa's village and a visit to Santa himself. And all this can be achieved in one day!

Notes

Chapter 1

p. 4   In Norse mythology Odin, the warrior god of wisdom and war: www.norselegends.com.

p. 4   Rudolph was created by the Montgomery Ward group: www.snoop.com.

p. 5   The smallest member of the deer family is the Pudu: G.K. Whitehead, *The Whitehead Encyclopedia of Deer* (Swan Hall Press, 1993), pp. 244 and 251.

p. 6   This complicated process involves a combination of four separate stomach chambers: *Black's Veterinary Dictionary* (A & C Black Ltd, 18th edition, 1995), pp. 480–1.

p. 8   The average reindeer stands 120cm at the shoulder: Whitehead, *Encyclopedia of Deer*, p. 246.

Chapter 2

p. 13   Antler shape has been used to split the genus Rangifer: N. Leader-Williams, *Reindeer of South Georgia* (Cambridge University Press, 1988), p. 4.

p. 18   In the summer of 1961: L. Miller *et al.*, 'Conservation of Peary Caribou based on a recalculation of the 1961 aerial survey on the Queen Elizabeth Islands, Arctic Canada', *Rangifer*, Special Issue No. 16 (2005): 65–75.

p. 19   The largest reindeer in Russia: Whitehead, *Encyclopedia of Deer*, p. 246.

pp. 20–1   Map of Distribution: Whitehead, *Encyclopedia of Deer*, p. 245; Leader-Williams, *Reindeer of South Georgia*, p. 5; A.W.F. Banfield, *A Revision of the Reindeer and Caribou, Genus Rangifer* (National Museum of Canada, 1961), pp. 46 and 77; D.R. Klein, 'Arctic ungulates at the northern edge of terrestrial life', *Rangifer*, 16 (2) (1996): 51–6; H. Røed, 'Refugal origin and postglacial colonization of holarctic reindeer and caribou', *Rangifer*, 25 (1) (2005).

Chapter 3

p. 24   wolves, by far the most important predators of caribou: Leader-Williams, *Reindeer of South Georgia*, p. 11.

p. 26   Although low in quantity, caribou milk is rich: E. Reimers, '*Rangifer* population ecology: a Scandinavian perspective', *Rangifer*, 17 (3) (1997): 105–18; C.M. Anderson and J.R. Luick, *Reindeer Husbandry and its Ecological Principles* (US Department of the Interior, 1968), p. 50; P.S. Zhigunov, *Reindeer Husbandry* (US

Department of the Interior, 1968), pp. 110–13; Whitehead, *Encyclopedia of Deer*, p. 134.

p. 29 Nutritious reindeer milk and good summer grazing: Anderson and Luick, *Reindeer Husbandry*, pp. 65–8; C.J. Petersson and B. Danell, 'Causes of variation in growth rate of reindeer calves', *Rangifer*, 13 (2) (1993): 105–16.

p. 33 When the caribou are unavailable in the summer: L.J. Jackson and P.T. Thacker, *Caribou and Reindeer Hunters of the Northern Hemisphere* (Ashgate Publishing, 1997), pp. 29 and 30.

Chapter 4

p. 34 The coat is made up of two types of hair: Anderson and Luick, *Reindeer Husbandry*, pp. 27–8.

p. 35 By inhibiting loss of heat through radiation: Whitehead, *Encyclopedia of Deer*, p. 87.

Chapter 5

p. 43 There are big differences between male and female reindeer and caribou: Leader-Williams, *Reindeer of South Georgia*, pp. 147–9.

p. 44 The green plants contain all the nutrients: Zhigunov, *Reindeer Husbandry*, p. 130.

p. 45 In certain areas the end of the summer also sees the fruiting bodies of mushrooms: Zhigunov, *Reindeer Husbandry*, p. 138.

p. 47 Lichens are widespread throughout the world: K.B. Boedijin, *Plants of the World* (Thames & Hudson, 1965), vol. 3, p. 215.

p. 47 The lichens generally preferred by reindeer and caribou: Anderson and Luick, *Reindeer Husbandry*, p. 75.

p. 48 Of the 16,000 species of lichen classified so far: Zhigunov, *Reindeer Husbandry*, p. 144.

p. 48 Until relatively recently it was assumed that all reindeer and caribou populations depended on a lichen-based diet: Leader-Williams, *Reindeer of South Georgia*, pp. 120–1.

p. 49 This depleted diet causes cravings: F.E. Zeuner, *A History of Domesticated Animals* (Hutchinsons & Co. Ltd, 1963), p. 119.

Chapter 6

p. 50 Whenever warmer, boreal forest phases prevailed: J. Clutton-Brock, *A Natural History of Domesticated Mammals* (Cambridge University Press, 1999), p. 11.

p. 52 Upper Palaeolithic people seem to have depended heavily upon reindeer: Zeuner, *Domesticated Animals*, p. 112.

p. 54 the early stages of such 'domestication': Clutton-Brock, *Domesticated Mammals*, p. 164; Zeuner, *Domesticated Animals*, p. 125.

p. 58 This has led to a school of thought among Russian scientists: P. Vitesby, *The Reindeer People* (HarperCollins, 2005), p. 26.

p. 58 Indeed the whole process of domestication: S. Budiansky, *The Covenant of the Wild* (Weidenfeld & Nicolson, 1994), pp. 51–2.

Chapter 7

p. 60 Paintings, thought to be 3,000 years old: M. Nieminen, 'Evolution and Taxonomy of the Genus Rangifer in Northern Europe', *Proceedings of the 2nd International Reindeer/Caribou Symposium*, Roros, Norway, 1979, pp. 379–81.

p. 60 More concrete evidence of reindeer domestication: B. Donahue, 'The Troubled Taiga', *Cultural Survival Quarterly*, 27.1 (2003), 37.

p. 61 It is unclear exactly where and when reindeer were first packed and ridden: S. Vainshtein, *Nomads of South Siberia* (Cambridge University Press, 1980), p. 141.

p. 61 The practice of riding reindeer was probably derived from horse culture: Zeuner, *Domesticated Animals*, p. 125.

p. 64 Direct suckling of milk from lactating females: Zeuner, *Domesticated Animals*, p. 127.

p. 65 It was not until the early eighteenth century that numbers of domesticated reindeer: I. Krupnik, *Arctic Adaptations* (University Press of New England, 1993), p. 162.

p. 66 Skins from reindeer slaughtered at different times of year: Krupnik, *Arctic Adaptations*, p. 176.

p. 68 Russian scientists looking at the process of domestication: Budiansky, *Covenant of the Wild*, pp. 95–8.

p. 68 Domesticated herds of reindeer show a substantial amount of colour variation: Sijti Jarnge and Gun. M. Utsi, *Bovtsen Guelmieh* (H.A. Trykk, 1994), pp. 57–68.

Chapter 8

p. 70 The indigenous people of the Arctic and sub-Arctic: www.raipon.net (Russian Association of Indigenous People of the North).

p. 71 Siberia is at the same latitudes: J. Forsyth, *A History of the Peoples of Siberia* (Cambridge University Press, 1992), p. 7.

p. 72 luxuries such as 'smudge fires': E.J. Lindgren, 'The Reindeer Tungus of Manchuria', *Journal of the Royal Central Asian Society*, vol. XXII (April 1935).

p. 74 Communal spirit was strong among these people: Forsyth, *Peoples of Siberia*, p. 50.

p. 75 The Chukchi could never be described as soft-hearted: H. Sverdrup, *Among the Tundra People* (University of California Press, 1978), p. 40.

p. 75 **However, the traditional dress of the Koryak included a wolf-fur hood**: G. Kennan, *Tent Life in Siberia* (Gibbs M. Smith, Inc., 1986), p. 171.

p. 79 **The most striking feature of their hunting techniques**: A. Spencer, *The Lapps* (David & Charles (Publishers) Ltd, 1978), p. 48.

p. 80 **Indeed, Shaman is a Tungus word**: P. Vitesby, *The Shaman* (Duncan Baird Publishers, 1995), pp. 34–5.

p. 81 **In a trance-induced dance**: Forsyth, *Peoples of Siberia*, p. 52.

p. 83 ***Nimat*, the sharing of hunted food**: Forsyth, *Peoples of Siberia*, p. 293.

p. 83 **With the recent change to a market economy**: www.raipon.net (Russian Association of Indigenous People of the North).

Chapter 9

p. 86 **Many of these indigenous peoples have lost their reindeer culture**: B. Donahue, 'The Troubled Taiga', *Cultural Survival Quarterly*, 56–8.

Chapter 10

p. 99 **Reindeer were introduced to more than thirty different locations**: Whitehead, *Encyclopedia of Deer*, pp. 306 and 307; Leader-Williams, *Reindeer of South Georgia*, pp. 19–31; F.L. Miller *et al.*, 'St Matthew Island reindeer crash revisited: their demise was not nigh – but then, why did they die?', *Rangifer*, Special Issue No. 16 (2005): 185–97.

p. 102 **Brought in by Norwegian whalers**: Leader-Williams, *Reindeer of South Georgia*, pp. 32–43.

p. 107 **Congress provided funds to implement the Reindeer Act**: A. Postell, *Where Did the Reindeer Come From?* (Amaknak Press, 1990), p. 85.

p. 107 **Reindeer herders lost anything between 75 and 100 per cent of their reindeer**: G.L. Finstad *et al.*, 'Conflicts between reindeer herding and an expanding caribou herd in Alaska', *Rangifer*, Special Issue No. 13 (1999): 33–7.

p. 108 **So it was that on Boxing Day 1929**: Postell, *Where Did the Reindeer Come From?*, p. 76.

p. 108 **These reindeer became the basis of the Canadian Reindeer Project**: G.T. Conaty and L. Binder, *The Reindeer Herders of the Mackenzie Delta* (Firefly Books, 2004), p. 14.

p. 109 **Pollyanna and the Submarine**: *Navy News*, March 2002.

Chapter 11

p. 113 **The First Reindeer**: Reindeer Council of the United Kingdom, annual reports, 1949–54.

p. 121 **Thus, since 1990 part of the herd has lived at . . . Glenlivet**: T. Smith, *Velvet Antlers, Velvet Noses* (Hodder & Stoughton, 1995), pp. 82–6.

p. 121 **the regeneration of native Caledonian pine trees**: G.R. Miller and R.P. Cummins, 'Regeneration of Scots Pine *Pinus sylvestris* at a Natural Tree-Line in the Cairngorm Mountains, Scotland', *Holarctic Ecology*, vol. 5, no. 1 (1982): 27–34.

Chapter 13

p. 133 **The last introduction of new blood was in 1995**: Smith, *Velvet Antlers, Velvet Noses*, pp. 162–8.

p. 137 **In Swedish Lapland today there are estimated to be 280,000 domesticated reindeer**: Swedish Board of Agriculture, *Reindeer Husbandry in Sweden* (2000).

Chapter 15

p. 156 **the red and white toadstool with hallucinogenic properties**: R. Highfield, *Can Reindeer Fly? The Science of Christmas* (Metro Books, 1998), p. 55.

p. 156 **'It has long been noted'**: N.N. Dikov, *Mysteries in the Rocks of Ancient Chukotka* (Nauka, 1971), p. 71.

p. 156 **It is well documented that reindeer are very partial to human urine**: Zeuner, *Domesticated Animals*, p. 119.

p. 156 **'The night-vessel, a large wooden bowl'**: Sverdrup, *Among the Tundra People*, p. 26.

p. 159 **The Coca-Cola company naturally likes to claim credit**: www.snopes.com.

p. 160 **Our Christmas Reindeer**: Smith, *Velvet Antlers, Velvet Noses*, pp. 14–19.

Chapter 16

p. 164 **vital routes, installations and pipelines are slumping**: M. Lynas, *High Tide* (Harper Perennial, 2005), pp. 41–2.

p. 164 **Russia's track record during the Soviet years was appalling**: www.raipon.net (Russian Association of Indigenous People of the North).

p. 164 **Atmospheric nuclear explosions, commonplace in the Arctic**: W.O. Pruitt, 'A New Caribou Problem', *The Beaver* (Winter 1962).

p. 165 **The Chernobyl nuclear accident of 1986**: V. Utsi, 'Effects of the Chernobyl Accident on Reindeer Husbandry in Sweden', *Polar Record*, no. 147 (September 1987).

p. 165 **Warmer summer conditions are likely to increase insect harassment**: H. Whitfield and D. Russell, 'Recent changes in seasonal variations of climate within the range of northern caribou populations', *Rangifer*, Special Issue No. 16 (2005): 11–18.

Bibliography

Anderson, Candy M. and Luick, Jack, R. *Reindeer Husbandry and Its Ecological Principles*, US Department of the Interior, 1968

Anderson, David G. *Identity and Ecology in Arctic Siberia*, Oxford University Press, 2000

Banfield, A.W.F. *A Revision of the Reindeer and Caribou, Genus Rangifer*, National Museum of Canada, 1961

Beach, Hugh. *A Year in Lapland*, Smithsonian Institution Press, 1993

Black's Veterinary Dictionary, A & C Black Ltd, 18th edition, 1995

Boedijin, K.B. *Plants of the World*, 3 vols, Thames & Hudson, 1965, vol. 3

Budiansky, Stephen. *The Covenant of the Wild*, Weidenfield & Nicolson, 1994

Chapman, Norman. *Deer*, Whittet Books Ltd, 1991

Chernov, Yu. I. *The Living Tundra*, Cambridge University Press, 1985

Clutton-Brock, Juliet. *A Natural History of Domesticated Mammals*, Cambridge University Press, 1999

Conaty, Gerald T. and Binder, Lloyd. *The Reindeer Herders of the Mackenzie Delta*, Firefly Books, 2004

Dikov, N.N. *Mysteries in the Rocks of Anciant Chukotka*, Nauka, 1971

Forsyth, James. *A History of the Peoples of Siberia*, Cambridge University Press, 1992

Hervey, Thomas K. *The Book of Christmas*, Wordsworth Editions Ltd, 2000

Highfield, Roger. *Can Reindeer Fly? The Science of Christmas*, Metro Books, 1998

Jackson, Lawrence J. and Thacker, Paul T. *Caribou and Reindeer Hunters of the Northern Hemisphere*, Ashgate Publishing Ltd, 1997

Jarnge, Sijti and Utsi, Gun M. *Bovtsen Guelmieh*, H.A. Trykk, 1994

Kennan, George. *Tent Life in Siberia*, Gibbs M. Smith, Inc., 1986

Krupnik, Igor. *Arctic Adaptations*, University Press of New England, 1993

Leader-Williams, N. *Reindeer of South Georgia*, Cambridge University Press, 1988

Lee, Richard B. and Daly, Richard. *The Cambridge Encyclopedia of Hunters and Gatherers*, Cambridge University Press, 1999

Lindgren, E.J and Utsi, M. *Reindeer Breeding in the British Empire*, The Royal Institute of International Affairs, 1948

Long, Douglas. *Global Warming*, Facts on File, 2004

Lynas, Mark. *High Tide*, Harper Perennial, 2005

Manker, Ernst. *People of the Eight Seasons*, Tre Tryckare, 1963

Manker, Ernst and Vorren, Ornulv. *Lapp Life and Culture*, London, New York, Toronto, 1962

Martin, Vance G. and Tyler, Nicholas. *The 5th World Wilderness Congress. Arctic Wilderness*, North American Press, 1996

Moore, Clement C. *The Night Before Christmas*, Running Press, 1998

Paine, Robert. *Herds of the Tundra*, Smithsonian Institution Press, 1994

Pielou, E.C. *After the Ice Age*, University of Chicago Press, 1991

Postell, Alice. *Where Did the Reindeer Come From?*, Amaknak Press, 1990

Russell, H. John. *The Nature of Caribou*, Greystone Books, 1998

Smirnova, Galina A. (compiler). *Fairy Tales of Siberian Folks*, Vital Publishers, 1992

Smith, Tilly. *Velvet Antlers, Velvet Noses*, Hodder & Stoughton, 1995

Spencer, Arthur. *The Lapps*, David & Charles (Publishers) Ltd, 1978

Sutcliffe, Anthony J. *On the track of Ice Age mammals*, British Museum (Natural History), 1985

Sverdrup, Harald. *Among the Tundra People*, University of California Press, 1978

Took, Roger. *Running with Reindeer*, John Murray Ltd, 2003

Vainshtein, Sevyan. *Nomads of South Siberia*, Cambridge University Press, 1980

Van Deusen, Kira. *Raven and the Rock*, University of Washington Press, 1999

Vitesby, Piers. *The Shaman*, Duncan Baird Publishers, 1995

——. *The Reindeer People*, HarperCollins, 2005

Whitehead, G. Kenneth. *The Whitehead Encyclopedia of Deer*, Swan Hall Press, 1993

Zeuner, F.E. *A History of Domesticated Animals*, Hutchinsons & Co. (Publishers) Ltd, 1963

Zhigunov, P.S. *Reindeer Husbandry*, US Department of the Interior, 1968

Ziker, John P. *Peoples of the Tundra*, Waveland Press, Inc., 2002

Index

Page numbers in *italics* refer to illustrations.